Selling Professional and Financial Services Handbook

Founded in 1807, John Wiley & Sons is the oldest independent publishing company in the United States. With offices in North America, Europe, Australia, and Asia, Wiley is globally committed to developing and marketing print and electronic products and services for our customers' professional and personal knowledge and understanding.

The Wiley Finance series contains books written specifically for finance and investment professionals as well as sophisticated individual investors and their financial advisors. Book topics range from portfolio management to e-commerce, risk management, financial engineering, valuation, and financial instrument analysis, as well as much more.

For a list of available titles, visit our website at www.WileyFinance.com.

Selling Professional and Financial Services Handbook

SCOTT PACZOSA
CHUCK PERUCHINI

WILEY

Published by John Wiley & Sons, Inc., Hoboken, New Jersey.
Published simultaneously in Canada.

For general information on our other products and services or for technical support, please
contact our Customer Care Department within the United States at (800) 762-2974, outside the United States at (317) 572-3993, or fax (317) 572-4002.

Wiley publishes in a variety of print and electronic formats and by print-on-demand. Some
material included with standard print versions of this book may not be included in e-books
or in print-on-demand. If this book refers to media such as a CD or DVD that is not
included in the version you purchased, you may download this material at http://booksup-
port.wiley.com. For more information about Wiley products, visit www.wiley.com.

Library of Congress Cataloging-in-Publication Data:

Paczosa, Scott.
  Selling professional and financial services handbook / Scott Paczosa, Chuck Peruchini.
    pages cm. — (Wiley finance)
Includes index.
ISBN 978-1-118-72814-7 (cloth); ISBN 978-1-118-72809-3 (ePDF);
ISBN 978-1-118-72844-4 (ePub)

1. Financial services industry. 2. Strategic planning. 3. Selling. I. Peruchini, Chuck.
II. Title.
HG173.P33 2013
332.1068′8–dc23
                                        2013029223
Printed in the United States of America.

10 9 8 7 6 5 4 3 2 1

To my kids: May you do great things and write your own stories someday

—Scott Paczosa

To the hundreds of clients, colleagues, and friends who have inspired my business life and influenced the thoughts presented in this book

—Chuck Peruchini

Contents

Preface

The strategic selling approach you are about to learn has been developed and proven in practice over a period of more than 20 years. The two of us have used it at five different professional services firms and in partnership with many more. It works better than any other method of selling professional services that we know of. Much better.

We developed this approach—now called the rock-ripple strategy—because we were dissatisfied with other ways we had tried. Getting results with those other methods required tons of sheer brute-force effort. We were banging the phones like madmen and it was burning us out. There had to be a way that was more effective and efficient, more suited to the new market conditions (which grow ever more difficult), more natural, and more human.

What we came up with is now in these pages. The principles and the process have been deployed by us in the field for years and this is the first time they've been put together in print so thoroughly. They can be applied to selling any type of professional service. And everything here is learnable, whether you are a sales veteran or a practitioner just starting to sell. The only prerequisite is a desire to grow revenue, dramatically, while serving clients better.

Acknowledgments

In developing this sales approach and this book, not only have we stood on the shoulders of giants, we've worked with a bunch of them. Many, many people have taught us key lessons about selling or helped us to see, at critical junctures, how to go forward: colleagues, clients, strategic partners, friends, and life partners. Naming everyone would be like trying to write the personal history of how Scott and Chuck became who they are. So let's confine it to this:

- First, when you read the many success stories in this book, please note that none are solely attributable to us. The rock-ripple strategic process is a highly collaborative process, even if you start out by trying it solo or in a small group (as we did). Results depend on getting ideas, feedback, and support for specific sales initiatives from trusted experts around you—including, of course, the practitioners or other in-house experts at your own firm. And thus it was with the rock-ripple successes we will describe here. All were made possible by the great people who collaborated on them at numerous firms over the years—most recently, at our present employer.

- Navigant has been pivotal in three ways. First, Navigant provided an ideal team environment for bringing the rock-ripple strategy to a high state of fruition. Second, Navigant serves clients in industries and environments that are complex, in flux, and facing numerous risks, who benefit from proactive strategic thinking on their behalf. Finally,—and this is essential—services sold by the business development team have been performed by the Navigant practitioners in a manner that makes clients very happy. You can't keep selling unless your company delivers!

- As for the book, Mike Vargo of Pittsburgh, a former journalist and now a freelance editor, worked closely with us on every aspect of planning, writing, and revising the manuscript.

- Authors of certain other books about selling have both informed and inspired us. You'll find a short of list of our favorite books by these individuals in Appendix A.

Finally, to everyone not named here: if we haven't yet expressed our gratitude personally, in a satisfactory form, we soon will.

Our only reservation would be if people ask us to treat them to a three-martini lunch. As the opening chapters of the book will make clear, practices of that kind—and the selling strategies that went with them—are now relics of the past. Times have changed. We hope this book will help you get off to a strong start on the future.

Scott Pacsoza
Chuck Peruchini
Chicago, 2013

A New Way to Sell

CHAPTER 1

Changing Times, a New Dimension: The Rock-Ripple Strategy

If you sell professional services, you deserve a battle ribbon just for trying. You are operating in a tougher sales environment than anyone has seen for decades.

And it wasn't supposed to be this way. From the 1980s and 1990s into the early 2000s, there were reasons to believe that the markets for almost every type of professional service—from consulting, legal, accounting, and financial services to public relations and engineering services and beyond—would keep growing. For one thing, companies were outsourcing more functions than ever. For another, these companies were beset by more forces of change than ever. New technologies, new business models and forms of finance were reshaping entire industries. Regulatory measures and public activism were putting new pressures on companies to respond.

It seemed that service firms could count on the bubbling cauldron of change to generate not only new business but recurring waves of new *kinds* of business. There were waves of class-action lawsuits to be litigated over issues from asbestos to shareholder rights. Government mandates were changing how companies of all kinds had to construct their buildings, keep their books, and handle data breaches. Globalization was leading fleets of companies into uncharted waters and so forth. The emerging age had all the earmarks of a long-term sellers' market for professional services.

What happened?

To many people the answer is obvious: "It's the economy." And certainly the new millennium has fed us a dreary diet of sluggish economic growth mixed with crashes and crises. When clients cut budgets, certainly it means fewer deals with more competition.

But a weak economy is only part of the story, and blaming the economy won't help you meet your targets. Nor does it point to a way of growing revenues despite the difficulties if you are an executive or equity owner of a service firm—despite the difficulties.

That's where this book comes in. We, the coauthors, take a more nuanced view of what has been happening. And we have a solution to offer: a proven strategic approach to finding and developing new business. It's one that can lead to dramatic, sustained growth in individual sales numbers and a firm's top-line revenue—even in hard economic times.

We have used this approach at multiple firms, over a span of more than 20 years. We've generated consistent big gains from it, right through severe dips in the economy. During a six-year period that included the recession of 2008–2010, we have exceeded ever increasing targets, often by very substantial margins.

Is it possible we've just been lucky? Or do we have a personal gift for selling, a secret sauce that can't be replicated? No, all evidence says the systematic approach is the key. We have trained team members in this approach, then watched their results take off as they grasped and applied the basic principles. The same approach has created major new revenue streams for corporate law firms that work with us. You can learn it and apply it in your firm.

IT'S ALL ABOUT RECOGNIZING CHANGE

The real secret is to begin by understanding the world that confronts us all today, with an eye to what has changed and what has not. Selling has become harder for reasons beyond a slow-growth economy. The nature of the selling environment has changed. Most notably:

- Budget cutting isn't just a matter of client companies spending less overall. There has been a shift in how they spend. They buy cautiously and selectively, ratcheting their choices down to items deemed urgent. Nice-to-have is dead and need-to-have is becoming more strictly defined.

- Not only do clients' budgets keep getting tighter, but also people's schedules are tighter. They won't take a meeting to listen to a standard sales pitch. Often, they will barely stay with you for a standard elevator pitch, tuning out by word number six.

- Sales relationships are more fluid and cannot be established or maintained as they once were. There is little chance to build personal rapport by socializing with clients, nor can you expect client loyalty based on your firm's past performance.

Given such changes, problems in selling come largely from failure to adapt. Methods that used to work for getting a foot in the door now draw blanks. Or if a door is open because a client has a clear and present need, you cannot make consistent sales by merely reacting to the opening. Others will get there at the same time, maybe sooner.

The selling approach you will learn about here succeeds, we believe, because it is strategically suited to today's environment.

- It is an approach that can get people's attention even when their minds and plates are full, *by giving them information worth listening to.*

- It is focused on selling high-need services to clients in high-need situations—clients who will buy your services in order to deal with new threats, requirements, or marketplace imperatives they are faced with.

- This brings us to something that hasn't changed: the persistence of change itself. There are still plenty of new business opportunities. They do indeed come along in ever-recurring waves because clients' industries are still highly subject to game-changing trends and events, which generate the waves.

- The approach that wins is a forward-looking, proactive approach, the kind presented here. You don't want to be fighting for position on the crest of a wave that is already full-force (and may soon begin to die down anyway). By doing some up-front work, of a type that we'll describe, it is possible to get in front of the wave. Then when it strikes, and doors are about to swing open, you'll be at the front of the line— top-of-mind with clients who are ready to buy.

No mystery, really. The approach has multiple aspects, but they all come together around a simple set of core principles. The rest of this chapter and the next will use some brief stories and examples to bring out the principles. From there we'll move on to the chapters that lay out specific steps for putting the principles into action.

Now let's hear a story.

WHAT THE MAN ON THE DOORSTEP DID

Getting the customer's attention has always been a classic challenge of selling. The phrase "foot in the door" comes from the time when many goods were actually sold by cold calling door to door. So here is how a modern-day seller at a doorstep succeeded at that task—despite a selling environment that, like yours, has gotten much tougher than it used to be—by using exactly the approach we recommend for selling professional services.

A friend of ours lives in an upper-income city neighborhood, a nice, quiet place with houses that have yards and trees. He says that during the years he has been there, many people have come to his door, but he has bought from only one of them.

The folks who did *not* make a sale included a lot of door-to-door types who now have almost vanished from the picture. Our friend can't recall the last time he saw someone selling magazine subscriptions ("You can buy those online now"), while home improvement contractors have learned that the people in our friend's neighborhood may be prime prospects, but they won't buy such a service from cold callers.

Solicitors for various causes and local merchants who are new to the area still come around. Our friend has mastered the art of interrupting at just the right moment to say, politely, that he doesn't have time to talk. "It's after the person's second complete sentence," he claims—at which point he'll accept any free literature the person has, tossing it on a pile of things to be read maybe never.

Then one day the doorbell rang in the late afternoon. There stood a man from a tree-service company, in his work uniform, with a truck parked nearby. Our friend was about to do his polite send-away routine until the man said: "Sorry to bother you, but I was up in your neighbor's tree across the street and I noticed your silver maple. Did you know it has a big dead branch that's going to drop? It looks like it could come down right on the corner of your roof."

Our friend stepped out to inspect the tree. His reaction was "Whoa, how did I not see that?" And, as the man proceeded to show him, directly in the line of the branch's probable descent were shingles, gutters, and a downspout. A break-and-bounce that went the wrong way might catch the chimney or wrap around to take out a window. Thus, a service was sold.

What drove this sales process? Significantly, the tree-company man made no explicit attempt to sell—not until after the need was confirmed, when he gave a quote for removing the branch and noted some other trimming that ought to be done.

The man initiated a sale by giving the client *vital and specific information*. He pointed out, and showed evidence of, a *potentially urgent need* of which the client *had not been aware*.

When you can deliver that kind of news, it is a door opener and more. It lays the foundation for the sale. And it lays the foundation for a whole ongoing strategy if you can do it systematically—as it turned out, the tree-company man did. He later told our friend that he repeatedly got jobs the way he'd gotten this one. When out working, he didn't just try to drum up new business by handing out business cards. He kept an eye out for critical situations brewing, and often spotted them.

He had especially learned to watch for patterns that could lead to multiple, repeated sales. For instance, silver maples are highly prone to "throw wood," that is, to shed weak or dying branches, so every yard with that type of tree got a close look.

This strategy, with some variations, is the same basic strategy we're inviting you to apply to your own selling process. In a nutshell: You learn a systematic way to detect and monitor emerging issues that could have unexpected impacts on clients' businesses. Then you become the bearer of the vital news, using it as a basis for getting and conducting meetings that lead to sales.

A skeptic might say: "Okay, the tree guy is able to spring vital news on homeowners because he's working with trees and looking at trees all the time and they aren't. The clients I'm after are experts in their industries. What are the chances of my telling them about any emerging issues they haven't seen coming?"

In fact, the chances are much higher than one would expect. Because of the very busy-ness of today's business world, clients across entire industries are often unaware of how events on the horizon could conspire to affect many of them. They aren't in position to see the waves taking shape, whereas you are.

Here is a rather dramatic example from our experience.

SENSE THE WAVE, TRACE THE RIPPLES

At the turn of 2007, our consulting firm was engaged by a nationwide subprime mortgage lender. The client company had come under federal scrutiny for its lending and accounting practices, and our consulting firm had highly on-point experience with such issues. During the U.S. housing bubble—which at that time had recently peaked—it was alleged the company had been making loans to borrowers who couldn't really afford them. In addition to the investigations, some borrowers were banding together to file class-action lawsuits. And though few recognized the larger implications at first, this was more than one company's problem.

We were able to detect the implications by taking a rather simple step: we looked for them. The lender had asked our firm to conduct an independent internal review, and while a team of specialists was busy doing that, we in our sales role had an eye on the class-action suits. We began keeping track of similar matters across the United States. None were earth-shaking, but the count was going up.

Digging further, we looked at national figures for the numbers of home-owners who were delinquent on their mortgage payments. The data were readily available to us and were an important lead indicator, since delinquencies typically precede foreclosures. In short, delinquency rates were going up. This suggested that the little wave we had spotted hadn't crested yet; there was a lot more in the pipeline. We widened our search and kept digging.

No rocket science is required for such work. We were just collecting bits and pieces of data, trying to see how they fit together. In this case they formed a picture that seemed to confirm an eerie hunch we'd been having. The pattern was reminiscent of the first scattered failures and warning signs in the early stages of the savings and loan crisis, years before. Now we were seeing the leading edge of the subprime mortgage crisis.

At that stage we didn't know how big it would eventually grow, only that it looked big enough to rock more than a few boats. The next question was: whose boats? Clearly any subprime lenders were at risk, but it was equally clear to us that the ripples could spread farther than their part of the pond.

We began reaching out to the firms we viewed to be affected, including a large international bank. There, we initiated a dialogue with a senior executive. We explained that some risks had come to our attention which might conceivably affect her company. She was skeptical but interested. She said, "You'll have to show me the risks." Then she agreed to a meeting.

We arrived with pages of summary data from our files, some of it news, some perhaps not. The key was that no one had put together all of the data points as we had. Additional meetings followed. Over time, the ripples we'd seen indeed reached the financial sector, with a vengeance. The bank mentioned above needed an independent firm to conduct a review into its own mortgage issues. Our experts were hired.

From this sale alone, our up-front research paid dividends. It enabled us to win a choice engagement over other firms, some of whom had done more historical work for this client than we had. It put us miles ahead of the ambulance-chasers who came crowding in once the need was widely apparent— as so many always do, into any scene, once it's too late for any of them to have a decent shot at demonstrating comparative advantage.

And, last but not least, our initial research and sales efforts paid long-term benefits. They put us in position to build an ongoing and expanding stream of sales as the issues evolved.

The kind of groundwork we did on the mortgage issue is a regular practice for us. It's based on a concept we call Rock-Ripple, which is by far the best route to sustainable sales growth that we have found.

THE ROCK-RIPPLE EFFECT

Rarely is it possible to grow revenues through a series of unrelated one-off sales. These are nice when they land in your lap, but in an environment where clients are hesitant to spend, you have to wait too long or work too hard for each deal. Sometimes you can get traction by trying to extend and grow a current line of business, but most people tend not to stretch that idea far enough. They confine themselves to going after clients or jobs that are essentially the same as ones they've already landed, only to find that the possibilities are limited or the window is closing on that type of work.

What's needed is a stretch into another dimension: ahead in time, much wider in scope. The idea behind rock-ripple is that disruptive events can open multitudes of new windows, and that's where growth will be found.

- Anything that disrupts or changes the conduct of business is like a rock thrown into a pond: it makes a splash.

- The firm(s) directly affected may have an immediate need for services, and if you can win some of the work, that's great. But there will be consequences rippling out in widening circles that affect many more entities.

- Therefore, it pays to ask questions such as: Who could be impacted? How? And how significantly?

At any given time, we have our sales team working on multiple different rock-ripple phenomena, at different stages of the cycle. Perhaps in one case, someone has just identified a case in which a rock has landed, while in other cases we are collecting data and evaluating whether to follow up, and in others still, we're informing clients and arranging meetings. Of course, there are many fine points to implementing a rock-ripple strategy. You will learn more about them in the chapters to come.

But to get there, we must first home in for a closer look at the modern business and sales environment. This will reveal why smart, experienced people are often unaware of the ripples headed their way (or at least, unaware of their full import). It will also make several things clear: the futility of traditional sales methods, why the approach we suggest is a natural strategic fit, and what the other pieces of the approach have to be.

CHAPTER 2

Fields of Vision,
New Relationships:
On Being a Guru

The selling environment seems to be fraught with paradox. Everybody talks about how fast the world of business moves and how quick you need to be to keep up. Yet when you go out to sell, it feels as if the process has never moved more slowly. There is more friction at every step, which makes it like trying to run in mud.

Deals take longer to find and longer to be signed. Clients delay their buying decisions, back-burnering any that don't cry out for attention like a gun to the head. Their companies have more internal controls and sign-offs required for every buy.

Many times, you may get the impression that clients just "don't see the need" they have for your firm's services or "don't see the value" the services would bring. Although that isn't always true, the impression comes close to the heart of the matter.

Even the smartest clients have limits to their field of vision. Despite all the tools designed to help them work faster and keep them posted on a wide range of issues, they have only so much time and attention to spend. As we will now show, they are caught in a multifaceted dilemma that can have profound consequences for them, and has utterly shifted the sales paradigm for professional services.

WHAT DOESN'T WORK; WHAT DOES

It's not hard to understand the competing demands for a client's attention, especially when considering the rapidly evolving information explosion.

Further, companies have cut staff to run leaner, leaving fewer people to do more work, while societal changes like the trend to more active parenting have encroached on people's schedules from another direction. If you try to get a late-afternoon meeting, you may hear, "Can't do it. Got to give a presentation, then run to take my kid to a soccer game." And the truth is that today's working parent would rather be at the game than sipping an after-work drink with you.

This has spelled the end to the old style of relationship selling, such as wining and dining clients or inviting them to play golf. It is no longer feasible to build *personal* relationships that way.

Relationships still count, however. Clients will buy from salespeople and firms they've gotten to know and believe they can rely on. What has changed is the basis of the bond that has to be forged. Instead of a personal bond, you must go directly to building a business bond, and even this cannot be done well by traditional methods.

Here is an approach that has stopped working, no matter how eloquently it is worded: "I'd like to come in and tell you about our firm. We've been serving your industry for many years, and if you will tell me some issues you're dealing with, I can show you what we'd advise." You are essentially asking the prospective client to start a relationship from scratch, on the client's time, for your benefit. Few will grant the luxury.

Somewhat more promising, maybe, is: "I know you're facing issue X right now. We have handled that sort of issue for a number of companies, so wouldn't it be worth your while to see what we can do for you?" Now you are offering specific expertise that addresses a present need. The fatal weakness is that many service firms offer similar expertise, which often makes it hard for the client to distinguish among them.

In baseball it's been said the key to hitting is just "see the ball, hit the ball," and likewise, in selling, "see the need, meet the need" makes sense. But when practiced as above it is purely a reactive strategy, which others can and will pursue, and therefore it puts you at risk of being perceived as a commodity provider. For firms that get cast in that role, batting averages are low.

Clients have to be shown a strong differentiating factor—one that offers a distinct benefit and gives them a compelling reason to establish a relationship with your firm. Practicing the rock-ripple strategy does this. *It puts you into a role that clients genuinely need.*

When people are busy, as most clients are, their perspective is necessarily both *shortened* and *narrowed*. They have so many pressing demands that they aren't left with much time to look for those ripples that might eventually strike them. People can also get trapped in functional silos. The tasks on their plate tend to be complex, with important details to be mastered. In that mode, they may not see the ripples rolling in from unexpected quarters, bringing either new threats or new opportunities.

You, meanwhile, are out interacting with people in other companies and industries. You have access to information that could impact many clients but that each of them, isolated by their individual concerns, will miss. Hence, you have the opportunity to take both a longer and a wider view of things, and to look for those ripples—noticing how seemingly unrelated events, or diverse pieces of data, might come together into a mosaic that shows the shape of things to come.

Then, when you bring that picture to clients, you are performing a service that is valuable in its own right. The grounds are laid for a *preferential* business relationship. Clients regard you not as just another service provider but also as a provider of strategic insights—in other words, as a guru.

BUILDING GURU STATUS

Wanting to have guru status may seem presumptuous or self-centered. Actually, it is another core concept of the approach we are describing here. The goal is to reposition yourself in the client's world. Over time, you become a trusted adviser. Both you and your firm come to be seen as expert sources of help with whatever may lie ahead. That is a very strong position from which to sell. It shifts the fundamental nature of the sales encounter in your favor.

And being a guru is an ongoing business. Sometimes we detect an emerging rock-ripple issue that rings a loud bell of urgency—and when we inform a targeted group of companies that might be affected, many quickly agree to meetings so they can hear more. This happened in 2011, when we noticed a changing pattern in the U.S. government's investigation of possible cases of waste or fraud in health care. We sent out targeted e-mails with a brief alert about what we were seeing. Nearly half resulted in face-to-face presentations or conference calls on the subject.

But usually the returns don't come in so quickly, or even directly, so we monitor the emerging issue and keep updating the clients on our target lists until the situation grows urgent enough to move them to act. Then come the meetings and sales. On some very long-running issues—the kind that build, or persist, over a period of years—we prepare newsletters summarizing recent trends and significant events. These are not mass mailings pumped out indiscriminately. Each newsletter goes to select firms and individuals, and we put care into each one. Recipients know they are being singled out to receive well-crafted synopses, which can't be had from the usual industry sources. We are building guru relationships.

Sooner or later, some of the recipients will call us. Or if we call them, they will know who we are. And recently, we received a call out of the blue from an individual who had not received anything from us. A friend had given him a copy of our newsletter about a particular chronic issue. He was sufficiently impressed that he called about services on *another* issue.

CREATIVE SOLUTIONS

Achieving guru status is more than a matter of spotting and reporting trends. The firm has to deliver solutions, and there are times when an off-the-shelf service package won't do. In those cases one can be a real guru only by coming up with creative, unique offerings.

Whenever you are able to do that, it harnesses and delivers the full power of the whole strategic approach. Here is a detailed example from our experience more than a decade ago.

The Asian economic crisis of 1997 sent ripple effects throughout the global economy. In rapidly growing countries across East Asia, demand evaporated and manufacturers were left with excess supplies of goods. When Asian steel companies released a flood of their metal onto world markets, driving down the price, steelmakers in the United States were hit especially hard. The U.S. companies also were facing increased competition from Latin America and Europe, and they had high costs per ton.

We were then at a Big Four firm. The people in our corporate-finance practice quickly saw how things were unfolding, so they were early to enter the resulting service market and came to dominate certain parts of it. The core offerings were restructuring and mergers and acquisitions (M&A) advisory services, for American companies wanting to take those standard routes toward viability for the long haul. But it was evident that more creative solutions were needed as well.

Steelmaking is a capital-intensive business. Squeezed by declining revenues and high operating costs, the companies urgently needed ready cash. As we, the co-authors, saw it, ways of improving near-term liquidity were at hand—if another major industry could be brought into the picture.

The steel industry buys huge amounts of coal, converting most of it to coke (a hotter-burning form of the fuel, used in blast furnaces). And the heaviest buyer of coal overall is the electric power industry, which was starting to be deregulated in the United States during the 1990s. We looked at the ripples from deregulation, seeing how they might intersect with the ripples troubling the steel industry. Then we made two suggestions:

1. We recommended that steelmakers and electric utilities form a purchasing pool for coal. This would enhance their contracting clout and reduce a key operating cost.
2. We also advised steelmakers to sell their company-owned electric generating stations to newly deregulated utilities. That would give the steel companies infusions of cash to service debt or complete acquisitions, while the utilities, now competing in open markets, could lock in steady captive customers by feeding the electricity right back to the steel plants year after year.

Since our firm could provide services to help the parties take such steps, it would all add up to a classic win-win-win. This proved to be the actual result, although not right away, nor exactly as we had proposed. Steelmakers and utilities didn't rush forward *en masse* to implement the suggestions. What ensued was more complex and drawn out, with different companies taking a variety of measures and then eventually moving on to face other challenges.

The one common thread is that we were now front and center in the thick of the action—building long-term relationships, selling a growing and evolving list of services to meet evolving needs—because the suggestions we had made went beyond what the client companies usually expected of service providers. We had done more than just try to sell them obvious add-ons to the restructuring and M&A services. We had brought them original ideas aimed at *expanding their scope of possibilities* in a tough time. Wouldn't anybody like to hear more? We thus went on to become, literally, their visionaries-on-call. And we won sustained business on that basis.

In today's world—where clients are hungry not only for cash but for ways to find strategic advantage in a changing environment—relationships cannot be forged or maintained on the basis of a prior track record. Relationships are only as strong as the ideas that keep them alive, and a true guru is a consistent idea provider.

WHAT'S NEXT?

Finally, to be a guru you've got to think like one. This work requires cultivating a particular mindset. We call it the "What's next?" mindset. The systematic, strategic process you will learn in the chapters ahead is cyclical and ongoing. All of the steps are constantly being renewed, repeated, and refined.

You want to be always scanning the horizon for rock-ripple events, even while you are building a sales initiative around a big one that you've just identified. And when each initiative moves to market you will be updating it regularly, giving clients fresh insights into the issue as it evolves, coming up with new ways to serve them as needed.

Essentially, the "What's next?" mindset is the mindset of a leader. Instead of feeling baffled and buffeted by market conditions, you are resolving to take the lead on changes in the marketplace. Instead of selling from behind the eight ball, you learn to sell from ahead of the game. You are truly taking charge of the sales process. It is actually exhilarating once you get the hang of it.

Does this approach require time and effort? Yes, but so do other ways of selling that are not nearly as effective. This one works for today's environment. Clients get what they really need. You get a strategy that puts you ahead in the race to catch, and ride, emerging waves of new business opportunities.

So there you have a brief tour of the basic concepts. To summarize, you've been introduced to a strategic sales approach that is centered around:

- Opening doors by pointing out, to clients, potentially urgent needs of which they had not been aware.

- Being able to deliver such news by focusing on rock-ripple effects.

- Building guru status by providing further insights and ideas.

- And constantly asking "What's next?" to keep the momentum going ever forward, ever upward.

By adapting this approach to your situation—and by executing it well—you can establish strong relationships and look forward to sustained sales growth. Now let's get started on the nuts and bolts.

CHAPTER 3

The Four-Stage Process: Why and How It Works

The strategic selling process that has worked so well for us has four stages: Identify, Evaluate, Innovate, and Deploy.

1. **Identify** rock-ripple events that could create waves of new business opportunities.
2. **Evaluate** whether a given opportunity is worth pursuing *for your firm*.
3. **Innovate** as needed, coming up with new solutions for clients and/or new ways to take the solutions to market.
4. **Deploy** the sales campaign.

How to execute this four-stage process, systematically and repeatedly, will be our subject from here on out. As Stephen Covey said, it's good to "begin with the end in mind," so let us begin by painting a clear picture of the end state that you'll be reaching for. Once all four stages are up and running well, here's what it can look like and why the up-front effort pays off.

WHY THE FIRST MOVER WINS

The goal is *to be ahead of the curve on emerging opportunities*. As we saw in Chapter 1, if you can be first in your market to inform clients of the ways a new issue might affect them, that is a powerful entrée—vastly different from being just another caller who shows up after the need is evident.

Furthermore, if you can then be first to actually win a sale and provide services for a new type of need, you gain a big edge in winning more projects of the same type. While competitors must try to show how their firms' past experience *could* apply to the new situation, you are able to speak with the force of first-hand knowledge. You have qualifications that others don't. That is a powerful edge.

The most chronic form of sales resistance that all of us face in professional services is not resistance to the new. It's the commoditizing effect: the tendency of clients to see all service firms of a given caliber as more or less equal. We coauthors have been very fortunate in our selling careers. We have worked collaboratively with world-class consulting talent. Unique talent can certainly be a differentiator; however, seldom in the brief space of a sales call can we make a case that our resources are inherently, dramatically different from those of other firms at our level.

So this sales approach becomes a key differentiator. We are not merely offering talent for hire. Working with our colleagues, we are doing something with it that adds value: investing our own efforts and drawing on our firm's expertise to get ahead of the curve *on behalf of the clients*.

When we warn them of emerging needs, our professionals are perceived in a new light; we're the gurus who saw it coming. When we can also win a couple of early assignments right around the time a wave of need is striking, the perception is reinforced immensely. Now we are battle-tested gurus who know exactly what needs to be done. This is both a source of value and reassurance to clients who may suddenly feel beset by unfamiliar forces.

And when we can be *consistently* ahead of the curve, therein lies the growth opportunity. Look at the graphs in Figures 3.1 and 3.2, which we'll proceed to explain.

In this selling approach, you are on the lookout for rock-ripple effects that could create *urgent* needs for *large numbers* of clients. Moving along the horizontal axis, time, in Figure 3.1, we see that an emerging issue typically simmers for a while before it has major impact. Perhaps regulatory changes are being proposed and debated; perhaps a crisis is brewing but hasn't broken out. There might be marketplace shifts affecting a few scattered firms, but not large numbers as yet—or maybe the ripples haven't yet spread to an industry where they will cause great upheaval.

Now move to Figure 3.2 and we'll see how the rock-ripple approach maps onto this picture.

You want to identify and evaluate the emerging issue while it is simmering, so you can innovate and be ready to deploy a selling effort in advance of the upsurge. Sales may not come right away, since it is hard to predict exactly when the issue will heat up enough to compel clients to act. You will,

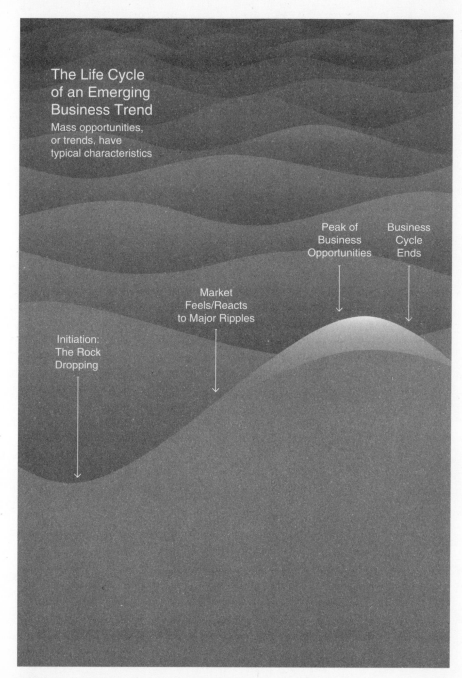

FIGURE 3.1   The Life Cycle of an Emerging Business Trend

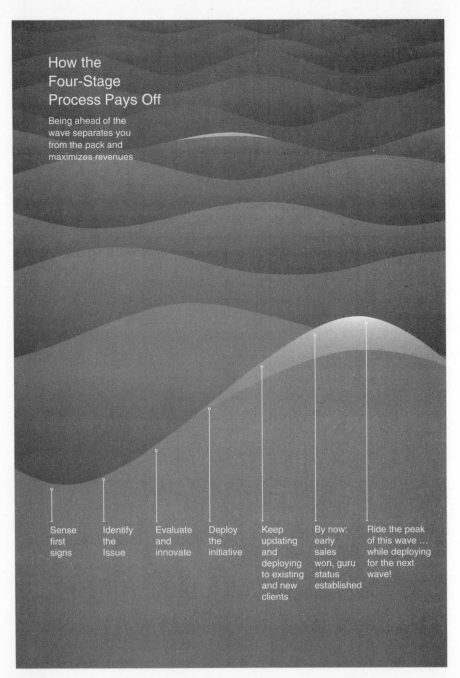

FIGURE 3.2   How the Four-Stage Process Pays Off

however, be prepared to win early. Then as the wave gathers momentum, so will you.

Competitors who take a reactive approach and come in later will win shares of the business. But to borrow a phrase from football: you have gained separation. You can be racing up the curve, leveraging your guru status, while they are scrambling for position.

Notice also in the graph that major business issues have finite life cycles. Think of the rush to comply with new standards or exploit any new market. There may be a period of sustained high need for services but eventually it tails off.

At a reactive firm, the sales force reacts as it always does, working harder to mine a dwindling stream of revenue from the old trend and hunting for anything to make up the shortfall, whereas you, by contrast, have been looking ahead: identifying and evaluating other emerging issues, innovating and deploying at the leading edges of those trends. This ever-renewing process—in which you are always looking for the next wave, and the next—pays off at the end of each business cycle as well.

As Figure 3.2 illustrates, when the current trend runs its course to the edge of the cliff, once again you will have gained separation. While other firms tumble, you are already leaping into new spheres of growth.

GETTING STARTED, FROM WHEREVER YOU MAY CURRENTLY BE

Now let's look at the four stages. The sections and chapters just ahead describe them as we have been practicing them, in a business-development unit at a large consulting firm, with access to a research department and other aids.

You may not have such assets. That is all right. You may even wish (or need) to learn the process on your own, as an individual within the firm, before trying to get broader buy-in to a new approach. That is how we began. One of us conceived this approach after being frustrated with the usual, just-work-it-harder approach to selling. Then the other came aboard and we began working as a duo.

Then as we tested and refined the process, and saw that it worked, we set out to institutionalize it in the firm: explaining and selling the process internally, teaching it to others, making it more systematic. You could follow a similar trajectory but can probably move faster from the start. The process doesn't have to be invented. You only need to adapt it to your circumstances—which could involve having an entire team learn and apply the process, from the start (and you can ask us to provide team coaching).

Or you may choose to go and remain solo. Further resources along with the book are available for that path, too.

Whatever the path, as you read the upcoming stage-by-stage summaries you should be able to see how our methods might transfer to your case. The more detailed chapters that follow include a number of suggestions on how to implement specific tasks either individually or across a firm, including in firms where the practitioners do the selling.

HOW THE STAGES WORK

Keeping in mind that the process repeats constantly—Identify, Evaluate, Innovate, Deploy. The first stage is to *Identify* opportunities.

Stage 1: Identify

With the onslaught of 24/7 business news plus instant analysis, one could say that everybody in today's society is being put on the watch for emerging trends and opportunities. The trouble is, there is so much information that people are overwhelmed. When you feel surrounded by endless chatter there's a tendency to pull back from it or screen it out.

But just as intelligence agents monitor many sources of chatter, and methodically home in on meaningful patterns that indicate something special is afoot, so does the intelligent seller of professional services.

The things that raise our eyebrows, prompting us to home in and start watching more closely, have the signature traits we've been talking about. They are:

- Events that look like they could be rock-ripples, impacting clients in *unexpected* or little-discussed ways. These are the facets of emerging trends that most people miss. They give us a chance to be early.

- Events that could impact an entire class or set of clients. Instead of chasing one-off projects, we are looking for multiple, related opportunities, around which we can build strategic initiatives and industrialize our go-to-market efforts.

- Events that would create an *urgent* or compelling need. Remember, nice-to-have is dead. This has to be something that would motivate clients to buy.

Also, we look for ripples generating types of work that it would make sense for our firm to pursue, given our capabilities and current portfolio. (For instance, would a typical project be roughly the "right" size? We don't want jobs so small that they wouldn't be cost-effective, but we don't want to get caught up in the volatile world of only whale hunting, either.)

Here is a story of how we homed in on a pattern that met all the criteria. A major issue in health care is cost containment. Given the expertise our firm could bring to the issue, we thought our best opportunities would lie in one aspect of cost reduction, investigations dealing with fraud and abuse in health care billing. So we started watching for new trends in government or private-sector efforts to target such overruns.

Among other things, we monitored activity by the Office of the Inspector General (OIG) in the U.S. Department of Health and Human Services. The OIG is charged with investigating fraud and abuse, and the staff members tend to work in "patterns." When they open a new area of investigation, it often means they've spotted a problem they think they can find in many places.

In 2009 we detected early signs of a new pattern. The OIG was looking into surgeries to implant cardiac-assist devices such as defibrillators in patients with heart problems. Growing numbers of these devices were being implanted, but were they always necessary? Was there proper documentation of the need?

In short, after evaluating, we developed our strategy and deployed an initiative. In this case, we saw that hospitals would be likely targets, since they bill Medicaid, and that it made sense to work with strategic partners. Over the next year, we won multiple projects from this initiative.

Formal and Informal Methods   The Identify stage has a couple of formal, structured components. One is regular close watching of specific information sources, such as the OIG. And to cast a wider net, we do periodic catch-up reviews. This simply means taking some time at defined intervals to comb through various source materials we haven't had a chance to track regularly. For instance, we scan selected web sites for posts that might offer clues to major events taking shape. Any item that looks fresh or significant is a data point.

Meanwhile, a number of informal processes are feeding into the mix. Every contact with a client is a chance to gather data. We make a habit of asking, often open-endedly, what clients are thinking about or concerned with. We also ask our practitioners what they're noticing out in the field.

Many times, these experts are the first to spot emerging opportunities or give us street-level verification of what our data points are suggesting. (And comments like, "Hey, we're starting to see a lot of that issue," will jump an idea straight to the stage of rigorous evaluation.)

Finally, we just read. We read the same publications many people read: the *Wall Street Journal*, business magazines, and so on. But we read with a special eye to identify.

Starting in August 2010, *Barron's* published a series of articles on Chinese reverse mergers. The reverse merger is a tactic that many companies in China, from high-tech start-ups to paper-products firms, had begun using to get listed on an American stock exchange (usually Nasdaq). A Chinese firm arranges to be acquired by a U.S. firm that is already listed but has become dormant, perhaps little more than a shell company. The Chinese "subsidiary" then announces that it is the new beating heart of this once-flagging enterprise, and can proceed to sell shares and raise capital publicly.

For some firms in China, a reverse merger can be a good way to grow, without the expense and work of going public from scratch. For others, it has been an avenue for fraud. Perhaps the Chinese company itself is only smoke and mirrors, a front for funneling investors' money into various pockets.

Having learned about this from *Barron's,* we started a formal tracking process as the news began to spread. The Securities and Exchange Commission investigated. Investors who'd been taken for a ride were filing lawsuits, not only against the phantom companies but against third-party service providers like the accounting firms that had audited them. We could foresee the ripples spreading further.

The punch line we want to leave you with is not the end of the story. It is an illustration of how valuable such an Identify exercise can be to a client or a strategic partner.

Shortly after, we had a conversation with an attorney at a major law firm. He had spent nearly three years immersed in a single complex case, and was facing a common dilemma: "Now I have to figure out how to get another client. What do I do?" It seemed the perfect occasion to share insights from our forward-looking rock-ripple strategy. We asked: "Well, have you looked at Chinese reverse mergers?" We pointed out that many of the legal issues and potential liabilities would be similar to those in the case he had been working on.

Moreover, we said, the impact of reverse merger cases was spreading. Our friend could find out who had been underwriting reverse mergers, or lending to the companies. Using what he learned, he could be at prospective clients' doors with a game plan before the wave struck them.

The attorney listened politely. Then he asked, "What exactly is a Chinese reverse merger?"

You may be surprised that a person at the top of the legal profession could have missed such news, but we were not. He'd been living in the world of his case. Anything unrelated to the case or to other pressing duties at his firm would have been a mere blip at the edge of the radar.

And this individual is hardly unusual. What is important is that we—and you—have an opportunity to connect the right dots and help watch the horizon on his behalf.

Stage 2: Evaluate

After identifying a rock-ripple wave, we have a good idea where to target future business. Now the task is to translate ideas to revenue. First, the idea must pass through a key filter, a formal evaluation.

The purpose of this stage is to decide whether further time and resources will be committed. It may be largely a matter of rechecking rough assessments made early in the Identify stage. Or, if a hot idea was fast-tracked up the chain, now is the time to examine it in earnest. We are trying to build a sound business case for a sales initiative (or to see that the case won't hold).

As before, we ask the basic questions: Would this wave affect a tranche of entities, not just a few? Would it create urgent needs, and would the jobs be in our firm's areas of expertise?

Our watchwords in the Evaluate stage are "consistent, robust analysis." This includes best-estimate calculating plus serious qualitative thinking about possible scenarios. We have done role-playing to get at how clients might respond to certain turns of events, and we always ask for input from our practitioners.

An important step is carefully "mapping" the opportunity to our firm. If the work would not map to our existing service lines, what would it take to develop new capabilities? How much investment would it take, and how would we then stack up against likely competitors? The core question here: given that this is a real opportunity, is it an opportunity *for us?*

Sometimes the answer is no. In one Evaluate project, we looked ahead to the time when U.S. business firms would have to comply with the International Financial Reporting Standards (IFRS) instead of the generally accepted accounting principles (GAAP) long used in the United States. Overall, the GAAP-to-IFRS transition promised to generate a lot of business. We analyzed how our consulting firm might participate and capture revenue. We sent a final analysis up to our own C-suite. The verdict: There simply wasn't an effective way we could compete with large accounting firms, so the idea died there.

Other times the answer is yes, and in fact it was yes in another standard-shifting situation. Hospitals and health care entities in the United States were given until January 2012 to adopt the World Health Organization's EDI 5010 standards. These are rules for coding diseases, symptoms, and other diagnostic information about patients into electronic file formats. Worldwide uniformity would help everybody, from physicians treating foreign travelers (and needing to look up their home-country health data) to epidemiologists studying disease patterns across countries. For the U.S. health care industry, the transition would be a giant headache.

Our firm had significant diagnostic coding expertise, and we determined that we could make a significant early entry. We had significant success from the early birds in the client universe who foresaw the urgency and acted promptly to buy transition services. Then, on the basis of that experience, we secured more assignments from the last-minute rush crowd. As January 2012 loomed, we had teams working overtime through the Christmas–New Year holidays.

The Evaluate stage can do more than stamp ideas with a flat yes or no. It can point us to the areas of an opportunity that suit us best. Since the first decade of the 2000s, data breaches over the Internet have become a major security issue. Criminal hackers rifle corporate databases for the credit card numbers and personal IDs of millions of customers. Industrial-spy hackers steal global competitive information. New forms of cybercrime and cyber-espionage evolve; the landscape keeps changing as attacks increase.

This was (and still is) a dynamic field, full of emerging, shifting needs. Many of the needs have to do with technology strategies for preventing or combating breaches. When we first identified the issue several years ago, we concluded that our firm could not help much there. We determined that we could, however, help a great deal with recovery from breaches, in areas such as being prepared to deal with the legal and business impacts. And that has become our domain.

Finally, evaluation can include trying to get a fix on the time frame of a new-business wave. Some emerging issues develop so quickly that the main question is how fast we can get to market. Conversely, others simmer for extended periods with no clear consensus about when or what the specific trigger event might be.

What we can do in such cases is to go on evaluating and preparing, so that when and if rocks begin to fall we are as ready as possible. Much of the time, we are more ready than the rest.

Stage 3: Innovate

In every initiative the stages of the process overlap somewhat. To properly identify emerging issues for the firm, we have to do some initial evaluating. A complete evaluation requires looking ahead to the service offering we could put together . . . and isn't that part of Innovate? Yes, it lays the foundations. Now let's consider what goes atop the foundations during the Innovate stage.

This is a time to nail down specifics and prepare to deploy.

It is also a time to add new or special twists to the strategy. (If you like strict definitions, this is the part that's truly "innovative.")

And our closing sequence—which can overlap into deploy—is the creation of a launch package.

Nailing down specifics includes an exercise called *targeting*. We target specific client companies (e.g., if we're going to sell to defense contractors, then which defense contractors?), as well as the firms with which we want to form strategic alliances. And of course, we refine and settle specifics of the service offerings. Creative twists may be added in any of these areas. Often, they involve new combinations that can *add value*. In Chapter 1 we described the idea of approaching steel companies and electric utilities to form purchasing pools and generation agreements. That combination was a win for all.

Strategic alliances are powerful combinations. They can be drawn up formally or based on a handshake, like one that we made for our data breach initiative, after we already had some client companies aboard. We had noticed that when our clients were hit with breaches, they always made the same series of phone calls. First they called their lawyers and us. Then they called a public relations firm. So we talked with the executive in charge of crisis management at a top-tier public relations agency. Essentially, we said: "We see you as a qualified and credible part of the solution required. We are in a position to recommend you. And there are times you can recommend our firm."

The result was a very simple alliance to grow new business for both, with nothing untoward in the bargain. Each party knows that the other is best-in-class and everyone wins, including the clients. (Indeed, "very simple" and "everyone wins" are often the hallmarks of successful combinations. A good bit of the innovative art lies in discovering these arrangements that seem so "natural" once they are made.)

The *launch package* for each initiative leaves little to chance. It is a well-defined strategy embodied in instructions and resources for the selling team. Our business development people are good at improvising, but they know that this form of creativity works best on the basis of being thoroughly prepared and briefed.

So we give them a turnkey package. Typical elements include a summary of the situation and strategy, a talk track—the core script to use with clients—and a list of the qualifications our firm has for a project..

There is much more to describe, and you will hear about it in the Innovate chapter. For instance, along with a selling campaign, we typically collaborate on marketing campaigns, with elements such as speaking opportunities for key professionals in the firm.

Stage 4: Deploy

Now it is time to go to market. How an initiative is deployed can vary greatly, depending in turn on any number of variables.

Initial feedback is one. Before cold-calling new clients, we usually roll out first to existing clients and strategic partners with whom we already have strong relationships (there may be certain exceptions to this, as we explain later). This reflects the value of the relationship, such that we give them first notice of an oncoming wave, *and* it is a chance to pilot-test the initiative with people who share our trust. Their responses may lead us to refine the way we sell the offering or alter the offering itself. Consistently negative responses could send the whole idea back for additional research.

The projected time span and scope of an emerging issue can determine the media we use to deploy. Recently, we detected a hot new issue that could affect firms in a particular industry niche. That gave us a focused target list and we set out to spread the alert promptly, using emails and phone calls to set up meetings. Data breach is at the other end of the spectrum. It is an ever-changing but persistent issue that poses ongoing threats to all sorts of firms. And it has called for a corresponding Deploy strategy, with features like quarterly marketing bulletins on the latest trends in data breach. The direct-selling effort persists over time, too, with new wrinkles (like the public relations alliance) added as they suggest themselves.

Also, in the course of any deployment, members of our business development team will come up with sales-pitch devices that work especially well. Many are anecdotes that drive home a selling point. We share these and tweak them—this is an official step in the routine, called developing anecdotes—so that everyone can build them into their standard talk tracks.

Thus, in numerous ways, we learn as we sell. The Deploy mode evolves as we execute, and the best evolutionary offshoots are institutionalized to make them stick. What makes this possible is a rigorous *tracking process*.

Following up on sales efforts is always essential, of course. For quite a while, we described Follow-Up as the fifth stage in our approach. We still like to state the need for it explicitly because, while sales professionals know that one has to track results, it's a function that tends to get dropped out by practitioners who sell!

The Deploy chapters will give specifics of the tracking process we suggest. Measurement and numbers are parts of the process, but please take note of the qualitative, human dimensions. In order to produce winning numbers, there has to be genuine human interaction about what is working or not, and why.

And the same holds true for the entire four-stage process. Put aside for a moment the formulas and routines. When you or the two of us go out to interact with clients, we are dealing with people caught up in human phenomena. They need *relationships* with people who can help them see what is coming their way, and then bring them solutions.

The four stages are a means of leveraging your ability to build these relationships—the kind that matter greatly in a turbulent world.

Stage 1: IDENTIFY

CHAPTER 4

The Identify Stage:
What to Look For

Now it is time for a closer treatment of the four stages. Before delving into stage 1, Identify, we'd like to suggest a particular way of thinking about the purpose of the whole exercise. Newcomers to our sales team have found this viewpoint helpful when they learn the stages:

> *The purpose of the four stages is to industrialize the selling process.*

• • •

Some people get the general meaning of this statement right away. If you are one of them, please stay with us while we trace it out more fully.

THE INDUSTRIAL MINDSET

Industrializing a process involves more than adding machinery or technology. Often, those steps are necessary, and in fact, you'll be using some simple technology tools in stage 1. But the tools are just a means to a larger end. When we industrialize a task—any task—we fundamentally change from one-off or piecemeal methods of working to an approach that seeks *high-volume results, consistently, at higher speed.*

And that's what you are being invited to do in the four-stage approach: industrialize the selling process. The approach takes some up-front work in terms of identifying and evaluating large-scale ideas on the horizon. But it is faster overall because once the up-front work is done, you can sell much more efficiently, reaping volume instead of chasing one-off encounters.

Here is an example that illustrates the point. Starting in 2007, the U.S. military's Special Operations Forces in Iraq adopted a new approach to fighting insurgency and terrorism. Devised by General Stanley McChrystal and his staff, the strategy proved to be very effective. One of McChrystal's officers called it "industrial-strength counterterrorism" because it literally industrialized the process of finding and closing down terrorist cells.

Early in the Iraq campaign, the cells had been raided one by one on the basis of leads gathered from intelligence. Essentially, whenever the forces had some clues to the location of a terrorist unit, they would go off and raid it, then come back to prepare for another raid. The tempo of operation was too slow this way. It could not keep up with the overall scale of the threat, and it gave insurgency leaders too much time to take evasive action if they suspected that visitors were due.

So McChrystal's command moved to a more scientific approach. They coordinated intelligence from multiple sources: surveillance aircraft, the monitoring of mobile phone traffic, news from human agents, and more. They sifted through all the data looking for *patterns* of activity by suspected insurgents—in part, by using methods of social network analysis adapted from civilian practice. With this up-front work they were able to develop maps of probable terrorist cells throughout an entire area of interest. Then soldiers could fan out to conduct multiple raids on the same day. And, after each one, they would immediately question captives and other people in the vicinity, often gaining new data that would help to lead to yet another location.

The result was pacification by mass production: a faster tempo, higher volume. McChrystal's strategy played a significant role in stabilizing Iraq to the point where troop withdrawal could begin.

• • •

Your mission is to sell services, not to pacify a troubled country at immense risk to your own life and health. Yet there are parallels in this example that apply to selling. In stage 1, Identify, you too will be collecting information from multiple sources, systematically. You too will be looking for patterns that add up to large-scale threats or needs. (In this case, they are needs that could affect large numbers of clients.) And then—once you have a clear idea as to the nature and distribution of a need, and the services you can offer—you will be able to conduct a very fast-paced and well-targeted, high-volume selling campaign.

On our sales team, a fully prepared business development person in the final stage of the four-stage cycle can make dozens of calls in a day, with a good percentage of them leading to face-to-face meetings. That is industrialized selling. We have seen it pay off in high-volume sales growth time and again.

Keeping in mind the value of industrialization, let's get into the specifics of stage 1. Everything that there is to learn about the Identify process can be broken into two categories: knowing what to look for, and knowing how to look. The rest of this chapter explores the what-to and the next chapter will deal with the how-to.

DEFINING AND THINKING ABOUT WHAT TO LOOK FOR

All of us are surrounded by incessant flows of information. The key is not to be overwhelmed, but to take in as much as you can while thinking about *how it relates to your business.* What is the significance of a particular event, in terms of how it might impact people you could serve?

To briefly recap the previous chapter, what you are seeking in the Identify stage are:

> *Events that will impact large numbers of identifiable parties in unexpected or little-discussed ways, creating urgent needs for services that your firm could provide.*

When all of the criteria converge, you have an idea that can be industrialized.

In the language we've introduced, you are looking for rock-ripple events. These always come from *changes* in the business environment. The initial change is a rock dropping—and whenever you notice such a change, *no matter in what sector of the economy or society the change might occur,* it is important to think about where the ripples could lead. You need to be always thinking critically about the events you come across, asking such questions as:

- *What are the implications of this change?* (And aside from the obvious implications: what else, what else?)
- *Which entities will be impacted?* Will it be certain kinds of firms, divisions or functions within firms, or groups of people . . . ?

■ *How will they be impacted?* Will they be placed at risk, forced to respond, or motivated to change their behavior . . . ?

■ *What fresh needs will this event create?*

Change can come in many forms. There can be sudden and fast-developing changes, such as the bursting of a market bubble, a major natural disaster, or a disruptive technology coming to market . . . and there can be slow-developing changes, such as social or demographic trends that will affect many businesses for years to come. Ideally, you want to see the change developing early (for instance, see that a bubble is likely to burst soon), which will allow you to get ahead of the curve in watching for ripple effects.

Some of the main categories of change, whether fast-moving or slow-moving, are changes in these areas:

■ *Global events.* Changes in international relations, or in business or political conditions in other countries, can impact anything from national security policy (and thus defense spending) to financial markets to the markets for almost any goods.

■ *Changing economic conditions.* And, as we shall see, it's important to keep an eye on regional as well as national trends.

■ *New legislation or regulatory rulings.* These are obvious game-changers, since they dictate what people can or cannot do, and they also may alter incentive structures (as with changes in tax laws).

■ *Technology.* Volumes have been written about the many impacts of technological change.

■ *Environmental issues.* These could range from new standards or trends (e.g., in the use of renewable energy) to disputes over practices like shale-gas drilling.

■ *Social changes.* When lifestyles or attitudes shift, or when people begin to care about new societal issues, the effects can ripple through the business environment in multiple ways. Spending patterns and buying habits can change; the kinds of laws and public policies that people support can change; and so on.

- *Demographic trends.* The aging of the population and the increase in immigrant population in some regions are examples of trends that can have far-reaching impacts.

- *Precedent-setting litigation.* Court decisions can impact businesses by expanding or limiting their exposure to tort liability, or to antitrust suits or shareholder suits, or by upholding or striking down local laws, and so forth.

From the scope of the list, it may seem there are far more changes in the world than anyone could possibly keep track of, in terms of identifying rock-ripple effects. But the watch list begins to narrow down rapidly when you test it against the initial criteria of what to look for, especially when you relate things to your firm's areas of expertise.

Consider environmental issues. Many U.S. cities now require that new buildings owned or funded by the city government must be LEED (Leadership in Energy and Environmental Design) certified for energy efficiency, and some cities have started including parts of the LEED standards in their building codes for *all* new structures. Many individual building clients as well want their projects built to LEED specs. This trend (and any new developments in it) would be of direct interest to architects, construction firms, and energy conservation consultants—whereas we, the coauthors, have thus far given the subject no stage 1 Identify attention to speak of.

Personally, we may care a great deal about saving energy. It's just that at the time the trend was growing, our consulting firm did no work related to green buildings, nor have we seen how any ripple effects from the green building movement could lead to large amounts of new business for us. But we certainly watch for environmental issues that might create such business. At the end of this chapter we'll tell a story of how one such issue, nuclear waste disposal, tied into a major new business idea. And the idea came from making a mental leap: we saw how the issue could be linked to the ripples from precedent-setting litigation in another field.

Looking for rock-ripple events requires stretching the mind in multiple directions. You have to be narrow-minded in the sense of focusing on changes that will trigger needs for your services, open-minded in the sense of being open to ideas that arise from unexpected quarters, and agile enough to make the connections between the two. Let's try a couple of thinking exercises.

EXPERIMENTS IN MIND STRETCHING

Following are three *obvious* examples of emerging trends. See if you can think of nonobvious ripples that might generate new business needs you could meet.

- In 2011, the first postwar Baby Boomers turned 65. Based on birth rates from 1946 into the 1960s, the numbers of Americans aged 65 or older will keep growing, dramatically, until at least 2030. There will be many ripple effects from this demographic shift. What are some ripples that might create opportunities for your firm?

- Advances in technology and the high-tech industries have been changing society in countless ways. Can you think of some ways that haven't been widely discussed, which create needs that your firm could meet?

- Economic growth does not occur uniformly. Typically, there are growth spurts and/or bubbles concentrated in certain industry sectors, and/or in certain regions. When these growth events happen, what are some ripples that could come your way? And, conversely, when regional economies are stifled or go into decline, this also can set off wide-ranging ripples. The 2011 tsunami in Japan damaged nuclear power plants, which prompted reconsideration of nuclear safety issues worldwide, and it disrupted the supply chains of Japanese automakers, sending ripple effects through the global auto industries. So think equally about how localized economic implosions could create service needs.

Again we invite you to stretch your thinking. For instance, yes, an aging population will need retirement services, and yes, growth in some parts of the Southwest has created demands for new housing developments and new public schools—but what else? Who stands either to benefit from, or to be threatened by, trends of this type? And what will they want to do; what will they need?

To show the range of possibilities, here are two actual examples of ripples that have spread from the trends just described. Both have provided waves of new business for service firms, and though the ripples are quite different in nature, both were driven by the same kinds of events.

Over recent decades, growth in several industries—notably high tech and finance—has produced new cohorts of very wealthy individuals. The entrepreneurs and investors in these fields have given the U.S. greater numbers of the "newly, truly rich" than at any time in any nation's history. And as these people grow into late middle age and beyond, many turn to the pursuit that wealthy entrepreneurs from John D. Rockefeller to Bill Gates have chosen. They feel a need to do good with the fortunes they have acquired and they become serious philanthropists.

The Bill and Melinda Gates Foundation, formed in 2000, is the largest private grant-making foundation, but far from the only new one. Thousands more were started around the same time, many of them small but also many of considerable size. Between 1990 and 2010, the total assets of charitable foundations in the United States nearly *quadrupled*. The trend shows no signs of ending, as additional tens of thousands of wealthy Boomers are expected to start foundations late in life, endow them in their wills, or at least seek professional advice to target their giving. Thus, demand has grown for a consulting service that barely existed until recent times: philanthropy consulting.

Service providers entering this area have included financial advisors, accountants, and attorneys, often partnered with field-of-giving experts who have left the staffs of existing nonprofits or NGOs. Some firms advise donors while others work on the development side, helping universities, hospitals, and the like to secure large gifts.

Meanwhile, at the same time that philanthropic activity was taking off, the same profusion of wealth created a surge in luxury homebuilding. And in affluent enclaves where land for new construction is scarce, a sub-ripple took shape. Teardowns became popular—the practice of buying a fine home in a prime location, then tearing it down to build a bigger one designed to the buyer's personal tastes. At the height of the hedge fund boom, this practice grew so common in the Connecticut towns near New York City that a local online news site began posting a feature called Teardown of the Day.

Architects and contractors with skills suited for luxury teardowns reaped a wave of new business. As a countertrend emerged, with townships putting limits and conditions on teardowns, there was business for lawyers, too. Then, eventually, in some places, the countertrend began to prevail. In 2010, Beverly Hills, California, passed a historic preservation ordinance making it very difficult to tear down older homes or buildings.

Our own feelings about teardowns are irrelevant here. The important point, for this discussion, is that such a ripple creates opportunities in certain regions *and so does the reaction to the ripple*. As the reaction grows, it can generate its own ripples, creating a different set of needs. Ordinances like the one in Beverly Hills will drive a demand for architects and contractors who are able to renovate within preservation guidelines.

DRAWING PARALLELS

Every year brings rock-ripple events that carry the seeds of industrial-scale sales ideas for all kinds of service firms. One way of learning to look for ripples of interest to your firm is to think about the kinds of events that drove waves of new business in the past. The same events won't happen again, but perhaps something similar will.

Suppose, for instance, that you have an executive search firm. A look into the past would tell you that two sources of large-scale opportunities have been (1) large numbers of executives and key professionals needing to relocate from a given region or industry sector, and (2) emerging demand for a new type of executive.

1. Not too many years ago, Long Island, New York, had thriving aerospace and electronics industries. Those regional industry clusters then shrank, as did the steel and heavy-manufacturing clusters in Pittsburgh. In both regions, waves of key people either were cut loose or were eager to jump to more promising situations. Some sought new positions in different industries close to home. Others migrated to areas on the West Coast or in the South, where their kinds of firms were growing and hiring.

   Whatever the path, search firms that moved in quickly were able to find *large numbers* of good candidates *urgently* wanting to be placed in new jobs. And therefore, in the future, it could pay to look for early signs of shifts in regional economic balance. These will be precursor events that may signal an upcoming need. Your firm could target likely prospects—including both new client firms in the growing sectors and new candidates in the shrinking sectors—and get in at the front of the next wave of matchmaking.

2. At one time the position called chief information officer (CIO) was unheard of. Then came a period when nearly every large organization saw the need for a good CIO. Similarly, the rise of venture capital, and later of private equity takeovers, created needs for interim executives willing to help launch a start-up or lead a turnaround. Changes in the health care system created demand for a new breed of hospital administrators with market-oriented competitive skills.

Are there industry trends today that could ratchet up the demand for a particular type of executive or skilled professional? Who would need these people? Where could you find them?

The same line of thinking can be applied to any service business. Basically, you are drawing parallels from the past as a guide to *what to look for* in the future. The preceding examples are fairly simple and straightforward. Not every new rock-ripple event will be a literal replay of one from the past with only the details changed. But by keeping your mind open to such parallels— and by getting into the habit of making analogies and associations—you can often direct your looking along avenues that prove to be valuable.

We will close with a true story from our own experience, which is slightly more complicated. In this case, we drew a parallel from one industry to another:

The story began with a rock dropping as a result of the savings-and-loan (S&L) crisis of the late 1980s and early 1990s. As the crisis grew, the U.S. government began looking for partners to help bail out failing institutions. One that stepped forward was the Winstar Corporation, formed by private investors to buy and run a troubled S&L in Minnesota. Winstar, like other buyers, was said to be drawn to the deal by the federal government's offer of favorable tax and accounting rules. These rules effectively bought time to turn the acquired S&L around, thus serving as an incentive while presumably serving the public interest.

But later the rules were changed. Winstar and others sued for damages. Our consulting firm provided services in connection with several of the suits. And we looked for ripples that could lead to similar business.

This brought us to a giant leap in thinking. We found an opening—an opportunity to apply the Winstar precedent—in an industry sector about as far removed from S&Ls as one could imagine: nuclear power.

For electric utilities with nuclear plants, disposal of the radioactive waste had long been a troublesome issue. An act of Congress, in 1982, had made disposal the responsibility of the U.S. Department of Energy (DoE). The DoE was mandated to provide one or more permanent repositories for high-level waste, such as spent fuel, by no later than 1998.

When 1998 came, no repository was available. The DoE had set out to build a vast underground storage facility beneath Yucca Mountain in Nevada, but for various reasons that project was (and still is) far from completion. Meanwhile, the utilities had been running up costs to store their spent fuel on site and to deal with related problems. Also, federal surcharge taxes on their customers' electric bills were being collected. Some of the money helped pay for the futile efforts at Yucca Mountain, while some went into federal coffers for no immediate purpose whatever. In light of the *Winstar* decision, might this also be an opportunity to provide our services? We thought so.

Eventually, numerous similar lawsuits were filed, and because of our experience and thoughtful positioning around the issue, numerous additional opportunities and revenue materialized for our firm.

• • •

To sum up this chapter: You are looking for rock-ripple events that can be turned into industrialized sales ideas. This requires active thinking and questioning, not "just looking." You will need to look across a wide spectrum but in a focused manner, making connections between disparate events and needs that your firm could meet. Drawing parallels from the past or from different industries can help guide you toward what to look for.

Next, we consider how to look systematically.

CHAPTER 5

The Identify Stage: How to Look Systematically

At this point we are getting into the actual, working details of the Identify process. You will be doing two sorts of things at the same time, a general looking and a more targeted looking.

THE ENTREPRENEURIAL MINDSET

The first consists of always keeping one's eyes and ears open. You never know where a critical piece of information might come from. Just in reading the news, or in a casual conversation, something could turn up that triggers a more rigorous Identify exercise. Or your reading or conversation might fill in a missing piece of the puzzle, and help you recognize an emerging pattern you hadn't spotted before.

Good entrepreneurs practice the art of keeping their eyes and ears open. Even when they are away from work, going shopping or to the gym, a part of their brains is always *on*—always relating what they see and hear to their business, always making associations that other people's minds normally do not. In this way, they may come up with an idea for a new product or just an idea that solves a nagging problem at work.

So you could describe this aspect of the process as adopting an entrepreneurial mindset. It is a reflective mindset but also an active mindset. You are attuned to opportunities to *create* business—filtering everything you see and hear, and sifting it for nuggets that can be put to use.

PUTTING YOURSELF IN THE PATH

Naturally, one also needs more focused methods of searching for information and ideas. Several such methods can be used in the Identify process. They all consist of narrowing in—*progressively* narrowing in—on specific sources that can give you initial ideas, and then take you deeper and deeper into the information you need to develop an idea.

At one law firm we know of, the general counsel realized the firm was doing a considerable amount of business across the food industry. It wasn't a designated practice area, but the firm had clients that included large farmers, a fast-food chain, and retail grocery businesses. So the firm joined a food-industry trade association, formally becoming part of that ecosystem. Partners and staff now had access to newsletters, bulletins, data services, and meetings of the trade group—multiple new sources of information to help them detect emerging trends and grow their food business further.

There are probably similar moves that any professional service firm could make. We call such a tactic "putting yourself in the path of information that is likely to matter." A related tactic, which can and should be practiced regularly as an integral part of the Identify process, is to target and channel information toward yourself, from highly relevant sources over the Internet.

TAPPING THE INTERNET

Nothing we are going to tell you here is earthshaking news. It is mostly a matter of using online tools and resources that are widely available, in many cases free of charge. Anyone can do what we are about to describe. Actually doing it makes all the difference in the world.

Whatever type of service firm you may have, you can make a list of online sources carrying information that is likely to matter to your own firm and/or to your clients. We do not know what the sources are, but you can sit down in front of a computer screen with some colleagues and generate a list.

Some might be general business news sites—anything from Reuters or Bloomberg to aggregator sites such as the Drudge Report or Huffington Post. Some sources might be aggregator sites for particular kinds of news (e.g., Slashdot for high-tech news). There are also the websites of government agencies—it's common for us to track a number of agencies, since we often look for rock-ripple effects stemming from regulatory changes or investigations—and the websites of other professional service firms that deal with industries and issues relevant to you.

For example, we make a practice of combing through the websites of major law firms. This is fertile ground for us for two reasons: (1) the material tends to be highly relevant to our business, and (2) attorneys are avid writers, turning out articles, memos, and newsletters on all manner of legal trends and topics. The firms post these on their public sites under headings such as "Bulletins" or "Insights," and they maintain very rich archives of past material as well as new items. One recent selection ranged from a summary report on legal developments in China to insights on changes in environmental regulation in the United States, to an analysis of a court decision on shareholder lawsuits over a leveraged buyout.

Better yet, for any subject, the law firm sites give us a mixture of inside news and expert opinion on the news, so we can see how both are trending. Perhaps these sites would be good for you to monitor as well. Or perhaps you know of equivalents to them, which would be more pertinent.

However you do it, the point is to (1) make a comprehensive list of likely information sources, and then (2) start monitoring those sources in a regular and focused fashion.

There are wide and growing varieties of online tools to help with the task. On some sites you can set up tickler alerts, to be e-mailed whenever news on selected topics arrives. Or you can use the software tools called newsreaders, RSS readers, and the like. With a little initial work to set them up, which any information technology savvy friend can assist you with, you get a personalized aggregator service fetching and displaying all the news on specified topics from the sources that you select.

And when do you go through all this information? There are no hard-and-fast rules for scheduling Identify sessions. In general, you want to check all sources frequently enough that emerging news items are still fresh when you see them, but there is no need to scan the Internet compulsively every hour or so. (Unless a major crisis is unfolding, that's probably a waste of time.)

We check our online news feeds once a day. Typically, one of us does it first thing in the morning, skimming quickly but attentively to pick out any items that might be of interest. Then we read those items more carefully whenever we have time, which may be later that day or in the evening. We also set aside blocks of time during the week to look at material that doesn't show up in the online feeds.

And regardless of how the day-to-day or week-to-week monitoring is performed, it is necessary to schedule periodic catch-up reviews, as mentioned in Chapter 3. These can be used to look at material that hasn't already been read or to follow up on particular leads.

If you are performing the Identify process as an individual or in a small firm without a small army of assistants, nearly all of this work will be in your hands. But don't worry—regular practice will make you efficient at the task, and you'll soon look forward to the thrill of discovering new business leads. In a larger firm with more resources at your command, you can delegate a good bit of the monitoring to researchers who will become your partners in the four-stage process. With sufficient resources you can also subscribe to paid data and news services, such as Factiva.

Either way, two key points apply.

1. As noted earlier, it's important to bring an active and critical mindset to reviewing and analyzing fresh information. This means actively thinking about the possible implications of what you read.
2. You will want to record any pertinent data that you gather. For example, once you think you have noticed an emerging trend, you will focus on it more sharply to start tracking it and gathering evidence. This evidence needs to be documented. Perhaps one company after another is experiencing a certain problem, and the incidents are being noted in the news or other sources. Perhaps an upswing or downswing in certain business statistics has prompted you to start looking for telltale trends in other, related statistics.

In all such cases you can build charts or tables that are updated with new entries as you find them. You can use standard spreadsheet files or any other software that lets you create the type of data-entry format you would prefer.

TAPPING HUMAN INTELLIGENCE

Along with searching online sources, the Identify process always includes the gathering of human intelligence. You need to be talking to people who are out in the field.

These people include your firm's practitioners, your clients, and strategic partners or other experts you trust. You can reach out to them to test or verify something you have deduced from your online sources. (We will give an example of this shortly.) And you can look to them as primary sources for leads and tips on what issues might be emerging.

Any personal encounter with human sources is a chance for an Identify discussion. Of course, it doesn't have to be announced as such. One simply asks questions like: What's new? What are you seeing? Anything unusual on your plate? Or: Here's what I have been noticing lately; what do you think? The process is a natural one. You are having a nonintimidating, friendly conversation in which you share information that could create value for everyone.

And the feedback you receive is vital. People in the field can help you gauge the relative importance of what you are finding or steer you in new directions if you are stuck. When you talk to them, you are taking your research beyond the limits of the ivory tower.

NARROWING DOWN AND HOMING IN: HOW THE IDENTIFY PROCESS COMES TOGETHER

The early signs of an industrial-scale idea may appear on your radar in any number of ways. But simply noticing that a big rock-ripple event is taking shape does not, in itself, tell you what you need to know. A big event can throw off ripples in many directions. The challenge is to home in on where the service opportunities would lie for your firm, and this work is really the essence of the Identify process. Since there are no standard rules for carrying out this part, we offer a description of how we typically do it.

Some rock-ripple events seem to defy analysis. They may present so many possibilities that you don't know where to begin. Or the initial signs may be just enough to persuade you that something big is about to happen, but not enough to point you toward a sure opportunity. The temptation is to table the matter for further discussion or thinking later, which in many cases translates to doing nothing.

There is an alternative to letting yourself be paralyzed. You can start from your firm's areas of expertise . . . trace out some possible ripples that lead in that direction . . . then test your thinking by talking to knowledgeable people, who can do two things for you: either validate your idea or shoot it down, and enlighten you as to where to look next.

We have done this many times in many different situations. Sometimes we share our tentative analysis with strategic partners who might be interested in pursuing the same ideas that we think we're seeing. Other times we test-market an idea with experts we know or with a select group of prospective clients. The conversation is usually along the lines of "We believe we see such-and-such headed your way, and here is what you could do to prepare for it"—with the latter often being a task that would bring our services into play. Then we ask for reactions.

Here is an example of the whole process unfolding:

In Chapter 1 we mentioned how, at the turn of 2007, we came to view the leading edge of the subprime mortgage crisis. Let us now sketch out the Identify process more completely. Our consulting firm was doing work for a nationwide subprime mortgage lender that had come under federal scrutiny for certain lending and accounting practices.

Since the housing bubble had just recently peaked, we reasoned that this was probably not an isolated case. With some initial research, we found that delinquency rates on home mortgages were rising—a sign of more trouble ahead, since delinquencies typically precede foreclosures.

Now we had enough to know that a major issue was probably on the horizon: a big rock was dropping. As with any big event, the ripples would spread far and wide. The question was: which would lead to the best opportunity for us? It had to be a high-revenue, industrial-scale opportunity suited to the kind of services we could offer, and preferably not a highly obvious idea, so that we could get an early lead on it.

Our data set at the time was thin. Nonetheless, the unique perspectives we had developed led to both outreach and then meetings with key industry participants. When we showed them the signs of the risk they were facing, they wanted to see more.

We went back and extended the Identify process to collect that evidence. Returning to these same clients, we obtained further meetings to present our new data. This made a sufficient impression that eventually, when the ripples did reach their doorstep, we were hired to conduct extensive reviews.

How far ahead of the curve were we? In retrospect, our Identify process gave us a margin of several months. Moreover, this work laid the foundation for significant additional business that has come our way since.

MOVING ON . . .

To sum up the story as it relates to the Identify stage: We started with an idea drawn from limited data and logical reasoning. Then we tested our thinking by taking it to people in the market. We were advised how to continue the Identify process, while also getting validation that it was worthwhile to continue.

And the story sums up the chapter by illustrating how Internet research, combined with human intelligence, can focus the Identify process until it narrows in on an industrial-strength business idea.

But there is much more to learn about the four-stage approach. The story that we just gave you barely mentioned the work we did in the second stage: Evaluate.

Typically, we evaluate an idea for business viability before even test marketing it. We do not want to begin selling until we are reasonably sure that we can deliver on the idea, compete on the idea, and earn a profit from the idea. You don't want to, either. That's what the Evaluate stage is all about, and we will tackle it next.

Stage 2: EVALUATE

CHAPTER **6**

Intro to Evaluation:
Basics and the First Step

The purpose of the Evaluate stage is to decide what to do about a trend you have identified. For that, you will need a deeper understanding of the kind of business opportunity it presents. The work consists of digging until you reach the depth and breadth of understanding required for a sound decision.

This entails research, but not the kind for which you need a PhD. The main ingredients are time and care. The stakes are high. You are choosing a course of action regarding what might or might not be a very large, high-paying opportunity. And a good evaluation can tell you a number of things.

It can tell you whether the opportunity is real and right for you.

It can tell you about the *nature* of the opportunity—to help you target your selling and help you decide what you're going to try to sell to whom, in order to have the best shot at beating the competition and getting high returns.

Also, in a good evaluation, you will look at what it would cost to go after the opportunity. (For instance, would you need to add staff or expertise? Develop a new service?) With a feel for the costs, you can then weigh them against the risks and potential rewards.

You can think of the evaluation process as being like the due diligence you would put into a major purchasing decision or a major decision of any kind. Before you buy into the opportunity, you want to be sure you're making the best possible choice.

Keep in mind that this is more than a simple yes or no decision. The Evaluate stage will lead to one of three basic types of possible conclusions:

- *Yes, and . . .* This means you will go forward, *and* you have narrowed in on details such as whom you will target with your selling, the solution(s) you would offer, and the investment and preparation you would need to make. (This is like a purchasing decision in which you conclude, "Yes, *and* here's what I want to buy, with these features and specifications, at such-and-such a price.")

- *No.* There can be various reasons for a definite no. Perhaps you consult some trusted sources and they show you that the idea is harebrained, unrealistic: the emerging opportunity you thought you had identified just isn't going to happen. Or a more detailed evaluation may show that the idea is a good one, but not for you. There are obstacles or draw-backs that would be deal-breakers and can't be gotten around.

- *Watch and wait.* Many of our evaluations come to this conclusion. We be-lieve that the idea we've studied has merit; we think a big sales opportunity is on the horizon, but it has not yet coalesced into a call to action. Similarly, in some purchasing decisions, you may have strong interest in an item but for whatever reasons, this is not the time to buy. Therefore, you keep an eye on the market until the right conditions are in place.

    When evaluating rock-ripple events, "Watch and wait" comes up fairly often because you have been trying to identify emerging trends, and it's not unusual to identify them before the time is ripe. Perhaps a big rock is about to drop but hasn't. Or, if it has, perhaps it is still too early to judge what patterns the ripples will take and where they will strike. Sometimes in our business, there has to be a secondary trigger event that will compel people to buy: clients are going to need our solution eventually, but it hasn't yet become a must-have, which means it would be premature to try to sell it. Therefore, we watch and wait—and prepare.

These are the possible outcomes of the Evaluate stage. Now let's go back to the beginning and see how an evaluation is done.

THE PROCESS: FIRST THINGS FIRST

At the start of an evaluation, you have some initial evidence. You think you've identified an emerging trend or event that will impact *large numbers* of identifiable parties, creating an *urgent* need for particular services that *your firm* can provide. You also think you are out ahead of the curve on this trend; you have a chance to get in early with an "industrialized" selling cam-paign that will generate a new, industrial-scale line of work for your firm.

This is your point of view on what is going to happen. It's like a hypothesis that a scientist forms, after some initial observations and thinking. What the scientist does then is test the hypothesis to see if it will hold up in the real world. That's what you need to do with your point of view. And the first step is *not* to attempt any sort of complex analysis with numbers and projections.

It is simply to take your point of view down from the ivory tower to the street, to see if your assumptions will hold water generally. We do this by talking with subject-matter experts who have firsthand knowledge of the market and are outside our firm. They may include trusted clients, partners, or friends in the industries in question. You have a similar set of people you can talk to.

We open a dialogue with these people, laying out our point of view and asking them what they think. The conversation doesn't have to be an hours-long grilling under a bare light bulb, but it is important to be thorough, touching on all the key points that would go into making this a legitimate opportunity.

Points we cover with the experts include:

- A basic reality check: Is this trend or event in fact likely to occur? Would it raise an issue that people in the marketplace really care about?

- Is the issue part of some larger trend?

- Who would be affected?

- Will this create multiple business opportunities?

- When the issue hits the streets, what will the affected parties be compelled to do?

- What is our solution? What can *we* do?

Essentially, in an evaluation dialogue of this type, you are talking through an entire scenario. You have come in with your version of how things would unfold; now you are testing it against the other persons' knowledge and getting their views on each point.

Of course, topics other than those listed may need to be discussed, such as the competition or special factors related to the issue. The goal is to get enough input to either *validate or revise* your point of view to a degree where you feel confident about moving on to the next step.

If the idea survives this first test, there is more evaluation to come. But some ideas do not survive. Here is an example of one that didn't.

LOST IN SPACE

In the late 1990s, we read an article about the commercialization of outer space. By that time, thousands of man-made satellites were in orbit around the earth and more were going up every year, many for scientific purposes, but also many for commercial use, such as telecom satellites. The most common orbital paths were getting so crowded that space junk was a growing problem. Satellites that had outlived their operating life would sometimes stay in orbit, along with objects like sections of booster rockets. Occasionally, newer satellites collided with them. This led to insurance claims and legal disputes—quite a few, apparently, because the article quoted lawyers talking about a burgeoning area of the law called space law.

All of this was news to us. And we figured it created an emerging need that mapped to services we could provide: our consulting firm had experts in areas such as quantification of damages. We were excited. Not only had we found a selling opportunity, we were going to lead the company into a new practice area that was literally out of this world!

The excitement didn't last long. After collecting a little more information, we took the idea to a couple of our in-house practitioners as well as trusted people outside. Yes, there were disputes and claims in outer space, they said, and the cases involved some work that our firm could do. However, the incidents were relatively few and far between; there just wasn't enough volume to merit a targeted campaign. Despite what some lawyers might have said to the news media, it was almost impossible to imagine the trend burgeoning to the extent that law firms or insurance firms would soon be desperately seeking space consultants.

Bottom line: space junk was, and is, a legitimate concern. Since the time we learned about it, international agreements have specified that satellites be rigged to shift into so-called graveyard orbits once their useful life is over, to reduce the risk of collisions. But in terms of *what the trend meant for our firm,* the idea that we had spotted a new industrial-scale opportunity was just a pie in the sky. And the very first step of the Evaluate process told us so.

OTHER POSSIBLE OUTCOMES

Just as the whole Evaluate stage is designed to give you more than a simple yes or no answer, the dialogues that you engage in to start the process can, themselves, produce outcomes other than "yes, let's go on to a deeper evaluation" or "no, the idea will never fly." Other outcomes may include:

- *We need to know more about this trend.* Initial talks with your street-level experts may not be enough to tell you whether you are onto something big. This leads to an iterative or evolving process, in which you go back to do more research, then come to your experts for another round of dialogue.

- *We're not ahead the curve, we're late.* Sometimes you learn that you have missed the rock-ripple. A trend that is news to you is not news to people in the affected area. They are already buying services from your competitors, who are out there selling actively.

  When this happens to us, we find that we have two things we need to do. One is to decide if we can still get into the market profitably, without burning a lot of effort on a low-batting-average catch-up campaign. We also look at our Identify process to see if there is anything we could have done better or differently. We want to learn from our misses.

Whatever the outcome, we stay committed to the rock-ripple approach and the four-stage process. It does not help to abandon it when the process gets difficult, or to lose heart when you miss an emerging trend. If we had done that, we would have reverted to one-off and commodity selling long ago—and we would have missed entire schools of fish (plus some pretty big whales) that we did manage to catch by sticking with the process.

NUMBERS VERSUS JUDGMENT

We also believe that feedback from experts is critically important to the Evaluate stage. There will be parts of the process that call for running some numbers, and those are important, too. Numbers, including projections of future performance, can be useful in several ways. For instance, if you bracket some ballpark projections and the most optimistic numbers tell you that a new opportunity still wouldn't be worth the investment, it probably isn't.

But it seems to us that the business world, in general, has become obsessed with quantitative analysis to the point where numbers are often used as a substitute for judgment. This can be especially dangerous when you are evaluating a new business opportunity. Many times, we have heard managers say things like "Give me a projection of the revenues"—and then watched them make decisions or deals, on the basis of those numbers, that did not work out. In retrospect, it often turns out that the estimates and calculations were made with due care, but were based on flawed assumptions about what would happen in the marketplace. Clients did not line up to buy the goods. They bought something else or deferred the purchase. Or they didn't buy at all, because they saw no need.

MOVING ON

Much of the rest of the Evaluate process is about seeing if you have a viable business case for a new opportunity. Some of it will entail ballpark estimating and calculating. But first you need the best possible answer to the most important question in any business case. Will there be business?

And if the goal is to sell on an industrial scale, the questions that matter most after that one are: Is it likely to be a lot of business (i.e., multiple projects of the same kind, not just an occasional one-off)? Who are the clients, and what will they need? Will they need it urgently? Can I sell it to them? Is this a strategic fit with the firm's direction?

All of these questions are purely or primarily qualitative, not quantitative. They're all about what the market is like and what the market is likely to do. They can be answered only by talking with people who know the market intimately.

Get the best input you can, then decide. And remember: it's okay to say no. You have only a finite amount of time to spend evaluating opportunities and only a finite amount of time to build campaigns and sell. You want to choose trends on which you can be ahead of the curve and go to market assertively. If you chase too many ideas that are not in your firm's sweet spot, you won't be cost-effective.

But if the verdict is that you have a live opportunity, it's time to move on to a deeper evaluation.

CHAPTER 7

Deeper Evaluation

Going deeper into a business opportunity actually consists of going deeper and broader. Just as the roots of a tree reach out around the tree to give it a firm foundation, this part of the evaluation includes reaching out around the opportunity into the various aspects of what would be involved in actually going forward with a selling campaign and winning the business, so that you can proceed on as firm a foundation as possible.

We'll spell out a list of the things that need to be evaluated and then give examples of how we did it, with some opportunities that we had identified.

EVALUATION POINTS

The following need to be examined and recorded—by this point you should be writing things out and generating files. Some of the main items will be things you've gone over before, in the Identify stage and the first part of Evaluate. Now you will look into them in more detail, nailing down specifics as much as possible.

Also, you are not done with your practitioners and other subject-matter experts. You may be calling on them for help with many of these items.

Start by confirming and examining the details of the rock-ripple sequence. And begin with the dropping of the rock—the trigger event that will create an urgent or compelling need. It could be either an actual, single event (like the enacting of a regulation that mandates clients to do something) or a confluence of events or forces. Either way:

- Has this trigger event already happened? (Or is it unfolding now?)

- If not, then when is it likely to?

- Is this inevitable? If not, best estimate of the likelihood?

- And likewise, where and when will the ripples strike, compelling people to take action?

If the compelling need isn't likely to be triggered any time soon, *which you can identify,* then put the idea onto the watch-and-wait track, and keep watching for the trigger event. You will probably still want to proceed with (and keep updating) a detailed evaluation to be as ready as possible. The trick is to go to market early—right at the front of the wave, before the competition—but not so far in advance of the actual need that people don't want to listen or will forget you by the time it arrives.

One more important note: Not only is it okay, it is in fact desirable, to have several opportunities percolating on watch-and-wait. We and our sales team are constantly in this state. Essentially, we have a *portfolio* of future business opportunities that are going to come ripe at different times. You want to be engaged in portfolio building, too. With several things queued up on the watch-and-wait track, you'll be constantly in action: taking an idea to market ahead of one wave . . . and then as you are starting to sell and build up guru status on that trend, it will be time to go to market with the next one.

Now let's come back to the evaluation process. The next items are:

Who will be impacted by this event? Will there be enough of them to make this an industrial-scale opportunity? And what will they need?

- As to who will be impacted: the important thing, at this stage, is to be sure you have an *identifiable* group of potential clients *and a means of identifying them and reaching them.* This may sound like an obvious thing to verify but we are spelling it out because it is essential. In the next stage, you will be targeting particular firms and people within the firms to whom to sell. You must know that you'll be able to determine who they are, and how to get to them.

- Will there be enough—in other words, will there be an entire school of fish that you can go out to catch (or a number of big whales)? We can't tell you exactly how many would be enough in a given case. Just keep in mind that you will not get them all, and there have to be enough so that with a respectable batting average, the campaign will be worthwhile.

- Finally, as to the services needed: be specific. Exactly how will the ripple affect the clients? Will it put them in a need-to-have, rather than a nice-to-have, situation? *Enumerate and describe* the services they'll need.

- Various clients may need different types or clusters of services, or at different times or on a different scale. If so, divide them into meaningful categories. Some may turn out be your prime prospects, some not.

How do these needs map to your firm?

- What are the services you could offer?

- If they'd be different for different clients, put them into the categories you've created. You may start to find that some map better than others, or look more promising.

- If your firm would have to add staff or otherwise gear up, see "Investment needed" below.

What is your differentiator? What will persuade people to buy from you, rather than from somebody else?

Now you get into seeing precisely what can or will distinguish you, and this is also where you get into analyzing both the competition and the clients' buying tendencies. So, again, be as specific as possible, enumerating and describing where needed:

- Will you be early enough to bring the news to clients or present it in a new and compelling way, thereby establishing guru status? What will be the nature of your pitch? (You can start generating or at least outlining your sales script here.)

- What are your firm's qualifications for the work?

- Who will be your likely competitors and are any of them onto this trend? How will you displace or preempt them?

- Do they have existing relationships with your targeted clients? How will you displace them or preempt them?

Furthermore, go back to your market experts for this aspect:
What can you learn about the clients' buying tendencies?

- Do they tend to be early adopters, last-minute rush buyers, in between?

- What do they tend to look for in choosing between service providers: comfort level, brand name, low price, leadership, speed of service ? How loyal are they to, or how dependent upon, existing service providers?

- What does any of this tell you about how to put together a selling campaign? What are the prospects of high-volume wins?

If you still believe you have a viable selling opportunity, take a closer look at what it will mean for your firm to actually perform the work.

What are the typical sizes of the projects that will result from sales?
Put down the best figures you can for each of the following:

- The approximate dollar value of a project.

- The ranges, if you will be offering different types or clusters of services.

- Your firm's targeted margins on this type of work.

What investment and preparation will be needed?
Will you need to add expertise, buy equipment, or make any other preparations to gear up or to be competitive?

- If so, enumerate and describe what will be required.

- Is it feasible to get, or do, what you need?

- What will be the rough cost?

- If the needs and costs will be different for different groups of clients, categorize them.

The numbers and needs you have projected will give you a picture of the feasibility, profitability, and desirability of the work.

Consider, also, that the future is uncertain:

Are there any external factors that could CHANGE anything you have evaluated and projected here?
If so, enumerate and describe them. And try to project the likelihood of key events turning out (or not turning out) as you expect them to.

When we run a formal evaluation, we are careful and thorough in assessing risks but we do not try to assign numerical probabilities to them (as in, we have a 60 percent certainty of being able to sell a particular service or add the expertise needed for the work). We simply list the things that have to be done or that have to happen and label the risk level for each as low, moderate, or high. The pattern that emerges will tell you the overall riskiness of going after the opportunity.

Finally, once you have addressed all of the points listed here, you should have a thorough enough evaluation to reach one of the decisions mentioned at the beginning of the last chapter:

- "Yes, we're going forward with this, *and* here are the details . . ."

- No.

- Watch and wait.

To show how the Evaluate process works in action, let's revisit three examples from our experience that were mentioned briefly earlier in the book. It would be too much to give you a full account of how we covered every bullet point on the evaluation list, for each of the opportunities. Instead, we will focus on the key considerations and findings that led to the decisions.

The first evaluation resulted in a "No." The second was a "Yes, and . . . ," which helped us target and refine our selling efforts. The third resulted in a "Yes" (and subsequent high-volume sales) for part of the opportunity, with the rest of the opportunity—which would be an even bigger part—put into watch-and-wait. You should see points that apply to your firm in each example, and at the end of each we'll share some general thoughts that definitely apply.

GETTING TO "NO"

In 2008, came an event that stirred great interest and much debate in the business world. The Securities and Exchange Commission (SEC) issued a proposed road map for requiring publicly traded firms in the United States to convert their accounting and reporting systems. The conversion from the generally accepted accounting principles (GAAP), long used in the United States, to the International Financial Reporting Standards (IFRS) coming into use worldwide would be a massive undertaking. As of this writing, several years later, the road map has been pushed back and no actual requirements have been set. But in 2008 it was perceived as a huge upcoming business opportunity, at least for firms providing accounting-related services.

Our consulting firm offers many related services, in areas from accounting to business process reengineering and change management, so it was imperative that we evaluate the opportunity, too. One thing evident from the start was that there was no way we could differentiate ourselves by being first to inform clients of what the impact could mean for them. The cat was out of the bag and everyone was talking about GAAP-to-IFRS implications.

All was not lost, though. Often, there are rock-ripple events in which the rock drops publicly. Sometimes, as in this situation, the potential ripple effects are fairly widely known, too. One can still catch the wave by going to market early and *strategically,* with well-chosen offerings that match your firm's strengths to the needs of particular market segments. A formal evaluation can show you how to do that. Thus, entry strategy became our focus with GAAP-to-IFRS.

Competitive analysis and market evaluation were crucial here. Clearly, we would be competing against major accounting firms, especially the Big Four. And the potential market (all U.S. firms that have publicly traded securities!) was vast and diverse. So we parceled the target market into categories, then mapped the needs and preferences of various kinds of clients to our firm's capabilities. What we came up with was a set of mismatches, as follows:

- Our firm was not well positioned to do a full-blown conversion; that is, a turnkey job of moving a client from GAAP to IFRS. We would have to add significant additional resources to compete on this. Then, no matter how good a job we did of recruiting top-notch individuals, we would have to sell clients on the notion that our quickly assembled team was on a par with firms whose teams had been working together longer.

- However, we were well equipped and positioned to do certain parts of the job. And a lot of clients would probably want a partial package, such as big multinationals that have in-house capabilities and would want to buy a set of supplemental services.

- Unfortunately, those big companies would be strongly predisposed to go with the Big Four accounting firms (and their consultancies) regardless.

They had long-standing auditor relationships with the Big Four and they were unlikely to see a compelling reason to switch for such an important task.

- Meanwhile, the midsized and smaller clients—who, we learned, would not be so automatically preinclined to use the Big Four—would be the ones most likely to need a turnkey conversion, which meant that the Big Four and other sizable accounting firms had an advantage in that niche, too.

Therefore, after much evaluation, the decision was a No. But the evaluation was worth doing. Some in the firm had wanted us to move straight into an IFRS campaign. This is understandable because a similar urge will come up any time a seemingly golden opportunity presents itself. Even if it looks like a stretch, people (or the voice inside your head) will say, "This one is too big to pass up. We can't afford not to be in it." In fact, what you cannot afford to do is to burn time and resources selling inefficiently.

Almost any industry-wide or multi-industry trend will probably have at least a couple of sales in it for everybody. But we have learned that if we chase opportunities that aren't right for us, that's about all we might get: a couple of sales in return for a lot of effort. The time we spend on formal evaluation more than pays for itself by steering us away from the uphill battles, toward areas where we can have a strategic edge and sell in volume, using our time productively.

A NOTE ON STRATEGY VERSUS SALES SKILLS

Sales is like fishing. There are two aspects to success. One is knowing where and when to fish; the other is knowing how to land the fish. Both are essential, yet most sales books and training courses focus on the second aspect: how to conduct and close a sale once you have a prospect on the line. While it is important to keep honing these selling skills, they are largely wasted if you talk to people who don't really need or prefer the bait you have to offer.

You want to find a place where there are plenty of fish eager to engage with you. It isn't necessarily where everyone else is fishing, nor does it do much good to head for a prime spot when the fish aren't feeding. Determining where and when to cast your line is the strategic aspect of selling, the part that puts you in a position to win consistently.

And most sales organizations do pay attention to strategy, just not always very effectively. At many firms the results of strategic sales efforts seem to come down to little more than fisherman's luck. What few have is a rigorous, repeatable strategic *process*. The four-stage approach, especially the Evaluate stage, provides such a process. Next is an example of how it paid off through ongoing evaluation.

"YES," PLUS CONTINUOUS IMPROVEMENT

Online data theft affects everyone. At this moment, hackers around the world are trying to steal your credit card numbers and personal ID. Data breaches grew gradually in scale and frequency from the mid-1990s into the 2000s, as malicious hacking evolved from being the work of occasional miscreants to an organized criminal activity.

In 2007 we decided to examine how and whether our firm could help with the problem. Early in the year, TJX, the owner of retail clothing chains including T.J. Maxx, disclosed that it was the victim of the largest corporate data breach to that time: the credit card information of more than 45 million customers had been stolen. The costs to TJX itself were huge. Other companies were experiencing thefts of trade secrets or business plans. The market for services was starting to boom.

When we sat down to evaluate, the first decision was which part or parts of the market to enter. Clients would have needs on both the protective side—for help with protecting against breaches—and on the recovery side, for assistance with all that comes after. Protection depends heavily on technology products and services, such as security software and the scanning of corporate information technology (IT) systems for vulnerabilities. Our firm certainly had expert IT capabilities, but it looked like this space would be dominated by IT-driven firms focused on technology enhancements.

During evaluation, we also saw a big risk in entering the protective side. Our consulting firm works in a number of areas where absolute reliability is the calling card, but it is impossible to give a client total security against data breaches. There are just too many ways for intruders to get in. They can find previously unknown flaws in systems, or exploit human errors by corporate staff, for instance. If we were to sell protective services and major breaches occurred on our watch, the reputational damage could hurt the rest of our business.

The recovery side looked more promising. Helping clients deal with unfortunate events is, generally, one of our specialties. And it turned out that with data breaches, there were *specific* needs that mapped directly to our strengths. When a company learns it has suffered a breach, an urgent set of tasks has to do with assessing and containing the damage: What exactly was stolen? How did it happen? What are the implications of this loss? What has to be done next? Are data still leaking? Who has to be notified? And so on. Our firm has expert forensic investigators and analysts and necessary related skills as well. Thus, we were able to get very clear on items such as which services to sell for which needs.

Yet an apparently simple item proved to be a stumbling block at first. We have emphasized in the Evaluate stage that you need to have identifiable parties to whom to sell, *with a means of identifying them*. So how does one identify parties needing post-data-breach services?

We thought we had a simple answer. We monitored the news. That didn't work well though, due to the inherent lag between a breach and public disclosure. First, the company has to discover that a crime has taken place; then the executives call outside counsel and other trusted advisers, to get their ducks lined up, as best they can; and only then does the news come out. (If it comes out at all. In cases where there is no requirement to notify others, the company may not.) Typically, we'd make contact only to learn that another service firm already had the work, through referral.

So, it was back to the Evaluate drawing board, looking for ways to be called or recommended as early as possible. We obtained some referrals through law firms. As noted in Chapter 3, we added to that by arranging for referrals through a public relations agency. Because data breach is an ongoing threat, we continued evaluating, and eventually we saw how to move further upstream in the referral chain.

In the emerging years of the threat and for quite a while after, it was rare for companies to carry insurance against data theft. Few insurers were writing policies, as they did not yet know how to quantify the risks. Only after 2010 did this market start to develop in earnest, but when it did, insurers began requiring their policyholders to have preapproved relationships with critical service providers, including forensic investigators. That was our signal to talk with insurance companies and get on *their* lists of preferred providers, so that clients can have our number in their speed-dials before they even suffer a breach.

Nor is that all. As the nature of the threats and responses keeps changing, we keep evaluating. A lot of what we learn goes into the newsletters we issue in parallel. Not only does evaluation provide the content, it helps us to target and retarget. We cannot be top-of-the-speed-dial with everybody, but we can try to stay top-of-mind with a good selection of prospects.

Over time, this use of a *consistent process* to constantly *iterate our selling efforts* has led to *dramatically* growing revenues from data breach services. We keep finding more and better places to fish.

EVERY STEP COUNTS

If there is a general lesson to be gleaned from this story, it is that every step in the Evaluate process matters. We believed we had an easy solution for one of them, and we didn't, and it turned out to be a key factor in the whole effort: finding the timeliest ways to identify and reach the clients.

The data breach market is so immense that it isn't feasible to canvass every potential client. Every firm or organization with an IT system is a target for hackers, and sooner or later virtually every one of them will have a breach: cyber security experts agree that it isn't a question of whether you will be victimized but when. The situation is analogous to a contractor's trying to sell emergency services for a trend that will affect "everyone who owns a building," or a public relations firm trying to sell damage-control services to every organization with an officer or board member who might do something embarrassing.

You want to focus your selling efforts for maximum yield and just following the first ambulance to the scene after the fact won't do the job, so where do you start? A careful step-by-step evaluation focused on *understanding how the market works* is always the best foundation.

It will lead you naturally into *segmenting* the market or targeting prime prospects in the most productive ways for your firm. Then you can keep building and extending the foundation as you sell.

"YES," PLUS ONE FOR THE PORTFOLIO

Our closing example, a brief one, is another standards-conversion opportunity that we mentioned earlier. Hospitals and other health care entities in the United States were going to be required by the Department of Health and Human Services (HHS) to migrate to the global International Classification of Diseases, Revision 10 (ICD-10) standards for recording diagnoses and other information about patients' health.

Our firm was very well equipped to provide the services needed for this conversion. And the potential market was very big. Evaluation showed that a key differentiator, for our firm, would be the ability to get in early. As with GAAP-to-IFRS, the ICD-10 issue was publicly discussed and we wouldn't be bringing the news to anybody, but early entry would enable our firm to build credentials quickly. On subsequent sales calls, we would be able to speak about ICD-10 projects with the force of first-hand experience, as opposed to just being qualified to do them—a world of difference—and that in itself would build guru status.

However, HHS had not yet issued firm mandates with deadlines for compliance. Thanks to a careful evaluation, we knew what preparations had to be made in order to be ready to move quickly, and we also had a good sense of how to time and stage the sales effort whenever the time was right.

As often happens with such matters, conversion to ICD-10 wound up proceeding in steps. HHS initially set deadlines for completing one part of the job: adoption of the so-called 5010 standards for exchanging data with insurance companies and others about claims, remittances, and so forth. Our firm was indeed able to sell and reap business in quantity from 5010 projects. From the evaluation process, we knew who the early adopters were likely to be and targeted them first. Then we went after more sales accordingly.

At this writing, the biggest part of the opportunity is still out there: conversion to the ICD-10 coding standards themselves. Tentative deadlines were proposed, then pushed back, and more than once. So we have that part on watch-and-wait. It's in the portfolio—along with other opportunities for which we are awaiting the trigger event that will create a must-have need.

And when it is time to go to market for the rest of the ICD-10 opportunity, our firm should be extremely well positioned. We will be able to start selling on the basis of the existing client relationships, and the guru status, that the firm established in doing quality work on the 5010 projects.

This story illustrates how the Evaluate stage can fit in with the entire four-stage sales approach, and with the underlying rock-ripple-guru concepts, to lead the way to sustained, high-volume sales and revenue.

Now let's move on to stage 3, Innovate.

Stage 3: INNOVATE

CHAPTER 8

Innovation and Preparation

In the Innovate stage, what exactly are you innovating? You are developing and refining two categories of things:

1. The solution, that is, the service offering(s) that you will take to market.
2. The sales campaign for the solution, with all of the sales tools, lists, and instructions needed. Some of the items will be familiar to you; some probably will not be.

This is also the stage when you bring the rest of your team on board. Unless you are working the entire four-stage process as an individual or in a small group, others in your firm will actually do much of the selling. Whether they are the salespeople under your leadership, or, in a firm without a sales staff, your fellow professionals, they are likely to know much less than you do about the idea you've been developing. They need to be educated on the issue and prepared to sell. The following pages will give you a series of steps for preparing them superbly. If you are working solo, you can still use most of the steps for preparing yourself.

Finally, the Innovate stage is the stage of moving into action, as it culminates with the launch of the campaign. The launch is always a dramatic event, and for us it is doubly dramatic. Whenever we see the pieces of a creative, well-planned initiative coming together in the hands of the team members who will bring it to life, we are reminded of how chaotic and difficult selling was before we discovered this process.

We started out in sales of professional services years ago, with the consulting arm of a major accounting firm. At first, we "succeeded" (i.e., more than made our numbers) largely by brute force. We just hit the phones relentlessly, jumping on every imaginable lead, tip, or hunch to make cold calls, warm calls, you name it. But eventually, we concluded we were on a dead-end path. We didn't want to try to sustain that kind of pace for a lifetime. Nor did we see much growth potential in the way we were selling. It wouldn't ever lead to significantly higher revenue unless we either put in more hours, which was impossible, or got lucky. And in any given sales period, luck could easily elude us or turn against us, because conditions in the marketplace change constantly.

That last fact led to the key insight. When changes are brewing, which they always are, would it be possible to get ahead of them and sell into waves of emerging needs? What evolved from there was a systematic method of doing so. As we'll show in this part of the book, it does more than increase sales. It lifts the act of selling to a different plane entirely.

Now let's move to the business ahead.

WHERE YOU STAND IN THE PROCESS

The four-stage process began in the Identify stage with a focus on what is happening in the market. During the Evaluate stage, you confirmed that a rock-ripple event is under way and got very clear on the nature of the needs it is likely to create. Also, a new focus started to come to the fore, as you started looking closely at *what you will take to market* and *how you will take it*. This new stage shifts the spotlight very intensely onto those subjects.

The need for constant awareness of what's happening in the market will remain ever present—in fact, your knowledge and analysis of it will become your chief calling card. But now you will be using that knowledge to shape, inform, and polish the goods you deliver. The first question is: have you got the right goods?

INNOVATING THE SOLUTION

In some sales initiatives, you can offer the clients an off-the-shelf solution. It appears from the evaluation that the needs they will have, as a result of the rock-ripple event, can be met nicely by a service that your firm routinely performs, or by some combination of them. You may think, essentially, "Wow, this plays right into our strengths. Everybody will need X and Y, which is exactly what we are good at." Thus, it may seem that your thinking on the topic is done—but not yet.

It is important to challenge your thinking and refine or sharpen the solution. Instead of assuming that the opportunity is tailor-made for you, are there ways to tailor your services—or your selling—to the opportunity?

The goal is to *differentiate* your firm as much as possible, by any means possible. Even if you are first to market and make a sterling impression as a guru, having spotted an emerging need, rarely will clients buy on the spot. The solution itself must be compelling, so it will stand out when clients compare it to what other firms are able to offer. It must also stand out later if you are to keep on selling through the crest of the wave, when the competition is out in full force.

Therefore, at this stage of the process, we always ask ourselves questions such as: Is our solution the *best* solution? Is it creative enough, in ways that reflect a deep understanding of the clients' needs? How could we enhance it, improve it, expand it? Could we, for instance, bundle our capabilities (or add new ones, or go to market with a strategic partner) so as to offer a more comprehensive solution, or a package that adds value in some fashion? Conversely, could we break out or customize some of the services to gain a lead in an important submarket?

The same type of questioning applies in situations where we do not have off-the-shelf solutions, and the firm must staff up or otherwise gear up for an opportunity. The major difference is that here the questions guide the process of constructing and fine-tuning a new solution that we had roughed out earlier.

In either case, the important thing is to ask a lot of such questions and examine them thoroughly. This is innovation with a purpose, the purpose being to capitalize on the opportunity as decisively as you can, by going to market with a true best-of-breed solution that gives clients reasons to choose *your* firm. Here are some examples from our experience:

- We described at the end of the previous chapter how we pursued the opportunity to help with conversion to the ICD-10 standards in health care. The government had set a deadline for ICD-10 compliance, but then deferred it indefinitely. Instead of waiting, we went after an earlier submarket for which a deadline did exist: hospitals and other entities needing to comply with the 5010 data standards. That entailed innovating a solution, in the sense of breaking out one set of services from the larger package that we had originally planned to bring to market. It didn't take a lot of effort, but it made a big difference. Simply by "meeting the need that was there," we were able to stake out a leadership position while gaining an initial revenue stream.

- Additionally, the data breach story in the preceding chapter was an example of innovating both a solution and a sales channel. Once the Evaluate stage showed that we were best suited to serve clients in investigating breaches after the fact, rather than in preventing them, innovation was still required in order to tailor our investigative services. Then, only with the passage of time were we able to find an "upstream" sales channel, through insurance firms that were starting to write data breach policies. When it is possible to innovate on both fronts from the outset—coming up with a tailored solution to an emerging mass need, as well as an inside-track sales channel—you have a very powerful combination.

Of course, we didn't invent the concept of innovating. Other service firms have innovated along similar lines, with good results. A spectacular example is that of H&R Block. The company was not conceived as a tax-return business. The cofounders, brothers Henry and Richard, had a storefront accounting firm in Kansas City. They did bookkeeping for local small businesses and, as a sideline, would usually prepare the owners' personal tax returns. Then a friend who worked in sales persuaded them to try something new. At his behest they took out a newspaper ad, offering the tax service to the general public at an affordable flat rate. The rest is history.

Moreover, H&R Block's good fortune was more than a matter of luck. It turned out that the friend had made his suggestion at a most strategic time. The year was 1955, the midst of the post–World War II economic boom. More individuals than ever were buying homes, making modest investments, and so forth. Their tax returns were getting complex, and they needed help. H&R Block capitalized on a massive rock-ripple effect.

Granted, not every firm can grow to be a multibillion-dollar multinational. But not many start smaller than a two-person accounting practice, either. The key point here is the universal applicability of the methods. Strategic innovation based on rock-ripple analysis can make a profound difference for any firm, of any size.

THE MULTILAYERED BENEFITS OF INNOVATION

Consider, too, the differences the four-stage process can make in a larger company such as ours. When we carry out the process, we are an integral part of choosing—and in many instances, helping to develop—the mix of services that we and our sales force are going to sell. This helps to set a strategic direction for the firm itself, not just for our sales team. And to some observers, that may seem a radical step. Doesn't it exceed the typical scope of a sales division?

Yes, it does, although in our view it is a natural step. The four-stage process elevates the sales management function to a better and more integrated role within a firm. There are industries in which it may be fitting to have sales reps who merely represent the makers of the goods, but professional services is not one of them. For us, using the process allows us to be what our sales team's official title says we are supposed to be: leaders of a *business development* unit. Our job is to study the markets, discover and understand what clients will need, and work closely with our practitioners to literally develop new lines of business for the firm to enter. In conjunction with the firm's leadership, we are adding colors to the strategic palette so that a more richly realized picture can be painted.

Over time, the results we have produced have made it easier to generate the internal support needed for a new initiative. Mastering the process can likewise prepare any sales manager for more of a leadership role. And there is an even larger benefit.

When you use the rock-ripple principle to identify new waves of needs, then innovate solutions to meet the needs, you are helping the firm to find its proper role within the marketplace. You are moving it into areas where its services fit best. The revenue then flows naturally, as it were, as an outcome of the fit.

Selling by this process does not eliminate the need for hard work, but in every respect it is a shift from struggling against the grain to going with the realities of the market, and having the realities work for you. You will see further evidence of the "naturalness" of the process in the next chapter.

Meanwhile, after you have innovated the solution to the best of your ability, you can move on to the details of the sales campaign.

INNOVATING THE CAMPAIGN

The steps here include creating and refining everything to be used in the campaign, from calling lists to the talk track for the sales call. We place a strong emphasis on refining, perhaps stronger than you are used to.

Each item needs to be as correct and as appropriate to the task as it can be, and as detailed and specific as it can be. Every person who goes out to sell should be as thoroughly well-armed and utterly prepared as possible.

The attention to detail will pay off for two good reasons. The first is well known by anyone who invents or creates for a living, which is that the best idea in the world may not work very well (or at all) unless it is implemented just right. You've probably heard the stories about Steve Jobs and his fanatical attention to every detail in each Apple product. Or perhaps you saw the news stories about the copy of the Mona Lisa that was discovered in 2012 by an art historian. The picture isn't a forgery; all the evidence says it was painted by a student of Da Vinci's, sitting next to the master at the same time he painted the original. The student's copy looks virtually identical at first glance: same woman, same pose, background, composition, everything. Yet it can't touch the masterpiece. Myriad *little* touches here and there are slightly off. They add up to the feel of the whole piece being slightly off, and as for the famous smile—well, it's a smile, and even the same kind of smile, but sorry. No sale.

The other reason for attention to detail is that you are creating an industrialized sales campaign to sell in volume. You want it to run smoothly and efficiently, like an assembly line in a factory, or a software program that you can plug and play. Of course, nobody building an assembly line or writing software hits it perfect on the initial pass. With either one there will be some debugging after the trial runs, and then adjustments or upgrades along the way. The same is true of a sales campaign. But it should not have so many flaws that it becomes like one of those tales that people from heavy industry tell, about the jinxed line that never gets up and running properly. The beauty of this approach is that when you get it on the money, it turns out a lot of money.

So let us proceed with a typical list of steps for developing the campaign.

BUILDING THE PACKAGE FOR THE SALES FORCE

Keep in mind that preparing a campaign includes preparing the people who are going to sell. From this point, we will assume you have a sales force (or fellow colleagues) who have to be brought in. If you are doing the entire process solo or in a small group working together, please just disregard any parts that don't apply.

We arm our salespeople with a complete package of materials that contains everything they will need to begin selling effectively. The pieces of this starter kit include:

- Background materials on the issue and the need.
- A targeted list of prospective clients for each person to call.
- Core messages and suggested "talk tracks" to use when calling.
- Information on our firm's qualifications for the work.
- Top-of-mind leave-behinds, which can also be distributed between calls.

All of these are described in the sections ahead.

All will be supplemented for the sales force, as well, by the discussions you will have during the launch call that closes the Innovate stage.

BACKGROUND MATERIALS

These are the first items on the list and the need for them should be apparent. Your sales force has to know what this new campaign is about. Clearly, you cannot tell them every detail you have learned, but you can pull together a basic briefing kit from your research on the subject. Pieces we put in for our people might include:

- News articles about the issue.
- Charts or tables we have compiled that show the direction of the emerging ripple.
- A brief overview of the client needs that are being created, and the solution(s) we will offer. This does not have to be artistically written, but it has to be specific and cover the main points.
- Any other summary materials that are *easily shareable* and that point to key opportunities or challenges likely to arise in the selling process.

We find that most of the above is easily obtained from what we have done in the Identify and Evaluate stages. Much of it, indeed, has already been developed and may only need to be assembled or cover-noted.

With background materials in place, we are ready to turn to actual selling materials.

TARGETING

We begin by targeting the people to whom we are going to sell, very precisely. The process here is one of homing in by levels of detail until you arrive at a template for an actual series of sales calls.

From the Evaluate stage, you should have at least a list of industries or market segments into which you are going to sell, plus a means of identifying the specific companies and people within companies who are targets. Within each company:

- Who is the person (or persons) to call? It must be someone who has buying authority. What is that person's title?

- Next, what is the person's name? Contact information? (Ideally, of course, you'll want both phone and e-mail, to try both as needed.)

- Also, is there anyone at your firm who knows the person, or has a connection to a connection, or knows an even better-situated person at the target company to talk to? Your firm may have a customer relationship management system or some other system that can be leveraged for this purpose; one can also just ask around. The purpose is to obtain information that will increase the chances of a successful approach.

You will be talking to the people on the target list about a rock-ripple event that will impact their business and create a need you intend to meet. Thus, what you can learn about where a company stands in terms of being susceptible to the event, or whether it has already been impacted by it, is also helpful. The purpose of the whole targeting exercise is to be as prepared as possible to engage the person who is experiencing the need.

Once you have target list, another consideration is who to call first. The order we often prefer is to test an approach first with some existing clients, particularly those with whom we have a "Hey, what do you think about this?" kind of relationship. It's fine to test ideas with them. We will also try it out on some prospective new clients, to see how it is received. We especially want to do this before rolling it out to existing clients who may have a low tolerance for any approach that is less than fully developed. You may want to triage your list similarly.

Based on all the information you've collected, you can also parcel out the list to your sales force, and once you have done so the targeting step is complete.

THE MESSAGE AND THE TALK TRACK

The next item is: what are you going to tell people when you call? The steps here are critical for arming your sales force. When we do this, our intent is that by the end of the Innovate stage our team will be as thoroughly pre-equipped as sellers ever were, so they can devote their time and energy to actual selling, through personal contact, with maximum productivity.

The task here is to map out the structure of the message you want to deliver, then script it into a suggested or sample talk track, with actual talking points.

This will be a different kind of message than the messages delivered in typical sales calls because this is a rock-ripple call. It will be a call that delivers useful news and content. You will start by apprising the client of impending impacts on his business and implications of which he might not be aware. You have to think about how to structure that crucial part of the message so the salespeople can communicate it concisely and clearly, and the prospective client can duly grasp its import and the needs that it will create.[1] This is where you begin to establish guru status.

And, of course, it also serves as the door-opener part of the message, just as in any sales call, but you now start putting the entire message into scripted talking points. Much of it will follow the classic progression of a sales encounter: You want to surface the need, elevate the need, and connect it to the solution you are offering.

Think also about what to say if you place the call and get a gatekeeper: the executive's assistant answers or you are put into voicemail. And consider that some clients are much more responsive to e-mails than to phone calls: You will want to draft a door-opener e-mail for those people.

---

[1] The exception would be if the situation is like one of those described in the preceding chapter, in which the impacts are already occurring or it's already apparent what the needs will be. In that case, you would still try to structure a message that conveys a distinct point of view on the subject or differentiates your firm in some way that will help position you as a guru.

We usually provide suggested scripts for a range of possible situations. Naturally, each salesperson will adapt our scripts into approaches that work for him or her. But the templates we develop are particularly valuable at the outset of the sales campaign. The salespeople don't yet know what is going to "work" for them, whereas we have a good feel from having tested the idea during evaluation.

When you finish the talk tracks, you will already have a formidable package of information to distribute to the sales force. Each person will be getting a briefing kit on the issue, an annotated list of prospective clients to call, plus a set of scripts to use. And there are more items to be added.

THE PROFESSIONAL TEAM AND QUALIFICATIONS

Two key questions:

- If the client were to hire your firm, who in the firm would be providing the services?

- What are your firm's qualifications for the work? This would include the experience and credentials of the key team members, the firm's history of doing such work, and other resources your firm could bring to bear on the client's needs.

When we do this part of the process, we ascertain and collect all relevant information right down to the curriculum vitae of the professionals who would actually perform the work.

We prepare a list of representative projects our firm has done—ideally, they are just like the jobs we are now trying to win, but we also include highly relevant or similar work.

We think about, and list, any other compelling qualifications we have (with qualifications meaning, literally, what it is about our firm that makes us eminently qualified for the job). And it all goes into the package for the sales force.

• • •

Next we come to a final set of tools to be created. Not only are these important, they involve a shift in thinking, so let us shift to a new chapter and begin afresh with them.

CHAPTER 9

Top-of-Mind Awareness Tools and Launch

It is customary to arm salespeople with collateral—pieces of literature they can use as leave-behinds or send as follow-ups. To quote from an online definition, this collateral "consists of materials that describe a business and its products and services."[1] The materials "include brochures, newsletters, fact sheets," and the like. In other words, it is a lot of stuff about the firm and its capabilities. Typically, the material is very slickly written and designed, so it will convey the best possible impression of the firm to clients. Or so the creators of the materials believe.

With rare exceptions, we don't use such collateral. For the follow-up role just described, we mostly create and use different kinds of materials, and there is nothing "collateral" about them in the sense of being ancillary to the purpose. Instead of giving clients collateral, we give them content.

Let us explain.

First, consider what clients really want, and need, to know. They do not want to learn about how great your firm is. They need to learn about the business issues that are confronting them.

Next, consider what your real purpose is in creating materials to give to clients after or between sales calls. You want to stay top-of-mind with them. You want them to think of your firm whenever a need arises, or becomes urgent enough to move them to buy, even if it is not during the course of the initial sales call (which it usually isn't).

Therefore, you will serve everyone's purposes best by providing useful content: real information about the real issues that affect the client.

---

[1] "Definition of Marketing Collateral," www.marigoldtech.com/dmglossary/glossary.php?term=Marketing%20Collateral.

The top-of-mind tools we rely on—which work exceedingly well—are of that nature. We have devoted a lot of time (and will continue devoting time!) to studying and tracking the emerging issues that we've built our sales campaigns around. So we digest the information into a useful and timely form to share with clients.

And most of the time, the form we choose is not a slick brochure or a bundle of information sheets with high production value. It is a presentable but rough-and-ready, easily updated form with high *content* value.

For example, we mentioned in Chapter 3 that we had built a sales initiative around services related to Chinese reverse merger cases. The basic thrust of our message to clients was: *More and more parties involved in these mergers are being investigated, then sued, when the mergers turn out to be questionable. You could be targeted next.* So, on an initial sales call, we would leave behind a printout from a spreadsheet file in which we had been tabulating and summarizing the progress of reverse-merger proceedings to date. It quite clearly illustrates the nature, scope, and trend of the threat.

But what about selling the firm and its expertise? We don't have to do that in words. We have demonstrated it. The clients will make the needed mental connection on their own—"Hey, here is a firm that's really on top of things"—and they will call when they have a need.

Often, in fact, they will call us about needs other than the one that was the subject of the outreach! We know we have a good campaign when it produces such indirect business in volumes equal to, or greater than, the direct responses. We will say more about this fortuitous side effect in the upcoming part on the Deploy stage. For now, we would like to leave you with the following points.

Whatever the subject of your sales campaign may be, you can produce top-of-mind follow-up tools. You have content in hand because of the research and analysis you have done. You only need to put it into *shareable forms useful to the client.*

Furthermore, if your firm does not have a dedicated sales force—if it is a firm where the practicing professionals must sell—these content-driven tools are easy to produce (no outside design agency required), *and* they are "natural" sales tools for practitioners to send and use. The practitioners aren't trying to use sales-y materials that might require them to learn about mysterious concepts such as unique selling propositions or positioning statements. A practitioner is supposed to be expert in the subject matter and the content simply reflects this. The message is the medium; the positioning is done, and it is the natural position that a serious practitioner would wish to communicate from.

PARALLEL MARKETING EFFORTS FOR PERSISTENT ISSUES

There is one type of situation in which we do send out professionally produced materials. These are the cases in which the rock-ripple event creates not just a one-time wave of need for services, but ongoing or recurring needs indefinitely. In the preceding chapter, we talked about the ongoing need for data breach services, and there are many similar sales opportunities with very long running life cycles.

A solid opportunity of this kind can be very important, of course, since it can generate sustained high-volume revenue. To capitalize on it, you will need a sustained sales initiative. And you may also want to plan a professional-quality marketing campaign, both to keep your firm top-of-mind and to sow the seeds for possible actual sales. We described the data breach newsletters that we issue. The newsletter format is certainly one vehicle that, at least for us, has produced very good results. It can be a reliable tool for anybody, as long as the newsletters are excellently done and truly useful to clients—containing, once again, *content* that can't be found or isn't pulled together in such a useful form elsewhere.

Other means of staying top-of-mind on an issue include booking speaking engagements for experts from your firm, and positioning them as sources to be called by the news media whenever they run a related story. The chief marketing person in your firm (or in an agency that you use) will, of course, know all of the options. If you educate this person on the issue and what you are trying to accomplish, a good marketing effort can be planned collaboratively.

● ● ●

Your campaign is now nearly prepared and ready to launch. You have assembled a complete package for the sales force, with:

- Background materials on the issue.
- Targeted calling lists.
- Messages and talk tracks.
- Information on the professional team and the firm's qualifications.
- Top-of-mind tools.

A parallel marketing campaign, if needed, is under way. All that remains before proceeding to launch is to attend to a few basic items from the sales-management perspective.

TARGETS, TRACKING, REPORTING

The following items would be part of any concerted sales effort. We are spelling them out to be sure they aren't dropped out here.

First, what are the targets you will set for the members of the sales force? For us, the metrics that matter are the number of meetings a salesperson gets as a result of the calls, and ultimately the dollars of revenue brought in. You may have other measures that you think are meaningful.

Now is also the time to plan how you will track and evaluate progress, and maintain communication with and among the team members. For instance, will you have a weekly meeting? And will the team use one of the online information-sharing tools that are now available? We do. Basic sales-package materials such as talk tracks and our inventory of the firm's qualifications are parked there; team members can also post results and stratagems that have helped them to *get* results. (You may recall, from Chapter 3, that we collect and share good anecdotes that our salespeople have come up with in order to drive home selling points.)

This online "team room" is valuable in multiple ways. It's a resource for continuous *improvement* of the campaign, as well as for coordination, and when new members join the team they can bring themselves up to speed quickly by visiting the room.

Finally, consider what your reporting-up requirements will be during the course of the campaign, and how you will meet them.

And now we come to the culminating steps of the Innovate stage.

THE LAUNCH CALL

This is the event where you bring together everyone who will be on the sales team, to explain and discuss everything needed to take the initiative to market. In some respects it is like the briefing before a mission, and in some respects it is like an initial public offering (IPO). You have put together your sales initiative with the kind of care and insight that would go into building a new company. Now it is about to literally go public.

Just as you would file a prospectus before launching an IPO, you distribute your sales package to the members of the sales force in advance of the launch call. It is their homework to read the materials and to be prepared with questions and/or suggestions. For our initiatives, we usually hold informal discussions with our salespeople before the launch call as well. They may know very little about this opportunity, whereas we have been living and breathing it. They need to be sold on why it is worth their while to commit to the initiative, and it helps to start winning hearts and minds, one person at a time, in advance.

The launch call itself can be held in any of a number of ways: as a physical meeting (if everyone is on site) or as a telephone conference call, a videoconference, or a Web conference. Here again, the content is more important than the medium.

We invite a senior professional or executive from our firm to participate. This is someone who knows the issue and the industries involved and will serve as our in-house expert on matters of substance during the call. Sometimes, if the occasion merits, we invite two such experts.

The launch call begins with a sales manager (i.e., one of us) outlining the initiative and "articulating the expectations"—that is, the time frame by which such-and-such results will be expected.

Then our senior expert provides additional background to the sales force about the issue. This person will cover topics such as the nature of the impacts on clients, the fittingness of the solutions we are going to offer, and what he or she thinks clients might be most responsive to when we go out to sell.

We—the sales managers who have prepared the initiative—will go into more depth on the sales hurdles and objections that are likely to surface. Typically, we have a good sense of these, both from our prior testing of the idea and from our personal experience in selling. Ideally, we are able to suggest strategies for overcoming major objections.

The floor is then open for questions and general interchange. At this point the launch call becomes a forum in which people can have things clarified and share ideas.

Also, members of the sales force will rehearse their pitches. This is a very useful exercise. It brings the initiative to life for everyone, and it serves the same purposes as rehearsing a scene from a play. People get to see how their lines come across. They can take suggestions and try variations.

If you are doing the four-stage process as an individual or in a small group, you'll want to come up with an adapted version of the launch call. For instance, you can still ask a trusted expert to sit with you for input and commentary on the initiative. You can practice your pitches with one another or with a knowledgeable friend. And you should by all means make expectations explicit.

A launch call typically lasts about an hour or more. The affair is very collegial, businesslike, and thorough. It is made clear that every facet of this initiative needs to be really sharp and that we have taken the time to assure that people are informed and equipped accordingly.

When the team members leave the launch call, they are ready to deploy an industrialized sales initiative. What comes next is the truly exciting part: you begin to see how your public offering will fare in the marketplace, and you will make the adjustments and enhancements needed to have it fare even better.

Stage 4: DEPLOY

CHAPTER 10

Transforming How You Sell: What's New, What Isn't

On the very first day that you and your salespeople pick up the phones to start selling, you will begin to notice *changes* taking hold. A casual observer who wanders through the office would probably miss them. To the uninitiated, it might appear to be just another day of business as usual, with various people in their characteristic talking-on-the-phone postures (planted intently at a desk, pacing back and forth, etc.) or tapping away at keyboards. But if you are actually doing it, it's another kind of ball game.

A rock-ripple deployment feels different and works differently from the usual sales efforts. As the campaign continues—and even more so, over time, as each new initiative dovetails with others you have launched—the differences multiply.

You should see dramatically better results. The ways that you get the results will be different, too. For instance, you are likely to have a lot more sales from unsolicited call-ins. And all of your sales will be the outcome of having built client relationships in a better and different manner than most people try. Instead of selling harder, you are selling smarter.

Moreover, you are selling smarter in a deeper sense than merely knowing some tricks that others may not. The approach feels different because you are *shifting the nature of the sales environment.* You are selling from a position of strength, as opposed to one of dependency and persuasion.

This part of the book is focused on the differences: the steps and principles that distinguish the Deploy stage of the four-stage process. There are a number of aspects to the deployment that are much the same as in any sales campaign, but we won't spend much time on them. In fact, it is worth a moment to note what these chapters will and will not deliver.

A GAME PLAN, NOT BASIC COACHING

We will not get into matters that rely on basic, individual selling skills, such as how to work from the talk track when making phone calls or how to conduct face-to-face meetings once you get them. These skills are important. Although selling should come more naturally with the strategic approach you are putting into action, you still have to know how to interact with potential clients, and there will still be times you have to overcome objections and know how to close a sale. We are assuming that you and any people working with you either have such basic skills or can learn them from other fine sources that are available.[1] What these chapters will provide is a superior framework within which to use the skills.

Much the same holds true for sales management issues. Chapter 12, which deals in part with building a sales team and culture, is a guide to cultivating the *particular* mindset and habits that are needed to maximize success with the four-stage process. But neither that chapter nor any remaining part of the book will deal much with universal matters such as motivating a sales force or working with employees who have personal challenges. Again, we assume that you can handle, or learn to handle, the basic tasks involved in leading a team of people. The present chapters provide the final elements of an overall game plan for the team. Executed faithfully, the plan will put each person in an optimum position to excel.

---

[1] For example, see Appendix A, a short list of books for further reading. These are books that, in our opinion, offer some good advice on how to conduct the selling process. They should also fit well with the four-stage rock-ripple strategy you are learning, because the books' authors share some basic philosophies that are closely in tune with ours. One is the rule that large, complex sales are won more by diagnosing and understanding the client's situation than by persuasion; another is that every sales encounter should, in itself, deliver value to the client in some way.

In short, this is where you merge your abilities with a strategic system for being more effective in the marketplace. Trusting the system will enable you to connect with new clients more effectively and go back to your existing contacts with greater effect as well.

So now let's look at how the game is played out. We will reclarify the objectives and then move to core principles and specifics.

WHAT YOU ARE SETTING OUT TO DO IN THE DEPLOY STAGE

You have just launched an industrialized sales initiative. It will be the first of many to come. The goal is to sell in volume, *increasing* volume, over a sustained period. And the initiative is designed to do so by giving you a distinctive platform from which to sell, based on the analysis you have done:

> *Having gotten on top of an emerging trend, you and your team are contacting a well-targeted list of prospects to give them valuable news and/or insights about upcoming needs. You thereby build guru status for your firm and build relationships that should lead to sales of the solutions you have in hand.*

This formula, which should be familiar by now, is one you will stay with. None of the precepts will change, only the specifics of how you implement them. For example, it's already been made clear that you will not be standing pat with your initial identification and analysis of an emerging ripple effect. As the campaign unfolds, new developments will arise: The issue itself will evolve. So you will stay abreast of the changes to keep generating updated analysis and insights, which you'll share regularly with clients in the top-of-mind materials described in the last chapter.

But deployment is more than a matter of just executing all the things we talked about in the Innovate stage. There are some new elements to be added, and some new angles to be aware of. Here are three major ones.

- *Events.* In addition to e-mailing top-of-mind materials to individual clients, you—or your salespeople, if this is a team campaign—will stage periodic top-of-mind *events*. Typical events are the roundtables that our team members put on, inviting groups of clients for discussion of issues pertinent to them (and to our sales initiatives). These events serve multiple purposes, as you will see.

- *Speaking to both sides of the client.* We have emphasized building relationships with clients on the basis of professional concerns, not by wining and dining them. But clients are people, and each client actually has two different kinds of professional concerns, relating to his or her *company* and *career.* This is good for you because it gives clients two sets of reasons for dealing with you: to acquire information and services that are useful to their companies and, in the process, to advance their own careers. We will say more about the power of using the sales approach in this book to speak to both kinds of goals.

- *Leveraging multiple initiatives.* Thus far, to keep things clear, we have described the four-stage process mostly in terms of how to develop a single strategic initiative. In reality, you will have many of them. And together the initiatives do more than add up. By being aware of how easy and natural it is to integrate them, you can achieve a multiplier effect over time.

We will also explain this last topic in some depth, as it is very important. Right now, it leads us to one more bit of stage setting (or, shall we say, mind setting) that is needed before getting down to the nuts and bolts of deployment.

TRANSFORMATION, NOT A BLITZ

What you do *not* have in the Deploy stage is a short-term blitz aimed at bringing in a lot of business in a hurry. It is nice when sales happen quickly, as they sometimes do, but this is not the norm in selling professional services, and it cannot be counted on. Even when you inform clients of an upcoming urgent need, most of them will not buy a solution until they actually feel the need and it becomes a priority for them: the proverbial gun to the head that can no longer be ignored.

Therefore, persistence in this context means something quite different than refusing to take no for an answer. It means staying on top of the emerging issue . . . staying top-of-mind with clients by updating them with useful content . . . and then, as a result of those efforts, being at the top of the list when they decide that it is time to buy.

When you and your team members follow such a trajectory, you are positioning yourselves distinctively in the market. Instead of being perceived as salespeople trying to make a sale, you (and, by extension, your firm) are seen as what you are: knowledgeable and well-prepared gurus striving to be of service.

You set the tone with your initial calls when you inform a client of an impending rock-ripple impact, or at least bring some helpful insights to the situation. Then you reinforce that with your follow-up materials and events. Everything you do acts in some way to position your firm as a guru on the subject, and every client contact places you in a role of serving the client in some way rather than being perceived as just trying to get something.

The process may take months before it leads to a sale; with some clients it may take a year or more. That is all right, as long you don't let the process lag. As the upcoming chapter will show, the key is to stay in a "what's next?" mode. What are the next steps you can take with this initiative? With each client? What is the next new initiative, and the next, that you can start to prepare? (Don't wait until the current campaign winds down!)

Soon, you will find that you are perpetually in a state of closing on the opportunities you have now, while laying the groundwork for future opportunities. This approach has a twofold benefit. It builds consistent growth and volume, taking the boom-and-bust volatility out of the selling function. And when the sales come, they come more naturally and profusely—both out of the relationships that have been built and out of the referrals and reputation you have gained concurrently.

Eventually, as we've said, you *transform the nature of the selling environment* in your favor. Within certain client communities where you are well known, your standing becomes that of a trusted member of, and adviser to, the community—a guru-in-residence. Clients literally bring their needs to you when they are ready. You are then able to sell from a position of responding to their needs, instead of trying to convince them to buy.

At our present firm, after conducting multiple initiatives over several years, we have reached a level where our indirect sales are at least as high as the direct. Whenever we launch an initiative aimed at a particular emerging need, we expect that at least half of the revenue will come from *other* needs. Some clients may not buy the specific solutions that we have offered them, but from having gotten to know us and appreciating our expertise, they will hire our firm for a different job. Or they might pass along the content-rich materials we have shared and we'll get calls out of the blue from clients who were not even on our calling lists.

For us, it has been an utter transformation from the state in which we functioned earlier in our careers: the state of desperately chasing one-off sales and working insanely hard to try and meet or beat our targets. Now a chief question is: How high can we set the growth bar for next year?

Such results depend on scrupulous execution and follow-up. Of course, they also depend on having a good firm able to back up your selling by doing top-notch work when hired. But we presume you've been reading this book because your firm deserves to have more business than your current sales methods can deliver.

The next chapter should put you on the way to functioning at a new level for the long term. It covers all the major elements of a full deployment, with multiple initiatives. As in previous chapters, the writing is directed to readers who have either a sales force or a team of fellow practitioners selling with them. If you are working alone or in a small group, most of what is said will apply equally well or can be adapted to your situation.

CHAPTER 11

Steps to Full Deployment

Having initiatives in full Deploy mode is like driving a car down the freeway. You might be doing a number of things at once—steering, accelerating, changing lanes, or turning onto new roads from time to time—and a lot more things are happening "under the hood" without your needing to attend to them each moment, and they all blend together seamlessly into a continuum of high-powered motion.

In this stage of the four-stage process, everything you do and experience becomes so interrelated that it's actually somewhat hard to separate it into categories. But for learning purposes, since it is stage 4, we can describe what you will be doing under four general headings:

1. Tracking, refining and extending the initiative.
2. Building client relationships, over time, by communicating about content through top-of-mind materials and events.
3. Extending relationships from one sales initiative into others.
4. Reaping indirect sales—that is, sales unrelated to the initiatives—as a result of building relationships and establishing guru status.

All of the activities involve teamwork, and we'll now address them in turn.

TRACKING, REFINING, AND EXTENDING THE INITIATIVE

While this is a process of building for the long term, the short term matters. Results can accrue over time only from doing what is needed each day. And while collaboration is essential, selling remains a competitive business, so in our initiatives we have a competitive element.

The initiative is launched with each salesperson working through his or her calling list. As noted in the Innovate section, the performance metric that matters most to us initially is the number of client meetings obtained. In addition to tracking those numbers against expectations, a couple of weeks in we have a calling competition, to see who can generate the *most* meetings.

Group calls or meetings with the selling team are scheduled every two weeks at first, perhaps once a month later on in the campaign. The purpose of these is to assess progress—not only by comparing numbers, but by comparing notes about what has worked well and what has not. Adjustments and enhancements can then be made.

At the level of detail, messages and tactics are constantly being tweaked. For instance, we have mentioned our practice of developing anecdotes, in which salespeople sharpen their pitches by sharing stories and anecdotes they've used for getting points across to clients. Moving up a notch to a more strategic level, the service offering itself may be tweaked or the campaign may be retargeted to some extent as we go along—either because market conditions have changed or because we are learning more about the market, or both.

Our practitioners, the people who will actually be performing the services (or *are* performing them, once sales are made), are kept closely apprised along with the sales team. Ideas and feedback are always flowing, especially early in the campaign.

The kinds of refinements that we've summarized briefly here are not exclusive to the Deploy stage of our process. They are typical of the continuous-improvement efforts one might make in any business process. A vast body of knowledge exists about how to keep getting better at things. You may have favorite methods you would like to apply, which could work well.

What is important is to make the efforts, and to institutionalize the idea of continuous improvement. There have to be regular meetings and practices. There has to be the expectation that the initiative will evolve in response to how the market responds.

We try to make each initiative as spot-on as it can be before launch, in every respect from issue analysis and targeting to the talk tracks. That work is necessary. It establishes the direction and brings team members on board with a clear understanding of the opportunity. It tells the clients we know and care about their issues and, to the extent we have it right, it will lead to sales.

But we also know that the fifteenth call a person makes will not be like the first. And after the third sales meeting, the initiative may begin to look significantly different than it did at launch. We expect to have a solid start, making strong first impressions and getting some initial meetings, then become increasingly effective as we go along.

WHAT'S NEXT, WHAT'S NEXT?

Now come some elements that are specific to a rock-ripple deployment. They have to do with staying top-of-mind and building relationships, which are the topics to be addressed in more detail shortly. Your team members must step forward in these areas, since all of them are interacting with their own groups of clients they hope to cultivate.

Your salespeople also are able to see how the emerging issue is playing out in the market. They learn how and whether clients are being impacted, and which aspects of the issue are the ones that clients are most eager to be updated on, or learn more about. In selling for our firm, for instance, we often build initiatives around issues that could put clients at risk. So, not surprisingly, we've found that the clients like to be kept posted on any relevant trends or patterns. They want to know how close to home the ripples are getting. They're looking for indicators that might set off their alarms.

There will be equivalent subjects of concern for the target clients in your initiative, whatever the issue may be. And for the clients in any given industry—whether they are bankers, builders, restaurants, or universities—there may be other emerging issues besides the one that you are proposing to help them with, which you learn about through contact with the industry.

Thus, your whole team needs to be constantly alert to what's next on several counts.

- Feedback from the field can help to shape the top-of-mind materials that you put together, to keep the initiative alive and growing.

- We also expect each salesperson on our teams to take the lead in organizing top-of-mind outreach activities, such as roundtable events, for the clients on their lists.

- Finally, *it is never too soon to start planning the next initiative*. If your current campaign is built around, say, helping people comply with a new set of requirements in their industry—and you find that rising costs or competitive pressures are of growing concern, and your firm could also help with that, in some fashion—maybe it's time to start an Evaluate process.

Keep in mind, too, that every initiative need not focus on a threat. Perhaps you see a compelling opportunity for clients to expand their business and grow, which carries with it an opportunity for you to provide services.

The common thread here is to always have new things in the pipeline. Once a campaign is launched, don't let it fade. Coming up with new ways to provide new information to clients will keep it fresh and moving forward, closer to eventual sales . . . and as you and your team adopt the forward-looking frame of mind, you will put yourselves in the zone of finding the seeds of the next wave, and the next. It is all about the power of what's next.

INITIATIVES MAY END, BUT THE PROCESS DOESN'T

A question arises here. When, and how, does an initiative come to an end? Or more precisely: how do you know when the time has come to terminate it? There is no standard answer. Often, the response from the marketplace will tell you. If you reach a stage where sustained best efforts are getting diminishing returns, it may be a sign to start scaling back and shifting resources elsewhere.

Usually, an initiative has a natural expected lifespan that depends on the nature of the issue. Some issues appear to be evergreen—the time may come when data breaches are no longer a worry, but we haven't seen it yet—while others involve crises or urgencies that are going to wind down. Also, the universe of clients that could possibly have a given need is finite. Once that market is saturated, or the firms are at least satisfied with where they stand, there won't be more business directly related to the need.

Such was the case with the shortest successful rock-ripple initiative we ever conducted. Some years ago, watching the news, we noticed that a rock had dropped. A beef processing plant was shut down because of an outbreak of salmonella. The shutdown was only temporary, until inspectors could verify that the problem had been cleaned up, but it left the owners of the plant in dire straits. They didn't have a backup facility to which to shift production. They were looking at a steep revenue loss, and worse, they would probably lose steady clients, who needed an ongoing supply.

The firm we were with at the time had a mergers and acquisitions (M&A) division. We wondered how many other beef processing businesses in the country were single-plant operations. Did they know the risk they were facing; might they be in the market for M&A services?

With rapid research, we identified about a dozen companies of the type. We called all of them. We found one taker. The owner was at a point where he had thought about cashing out of the business anyway, and this struck him as a good time to sell it, before something happened to ruin its value. So our firm arranged the divestiture of his beef plant to a consolidator. Our firm earned a sizable commission on the deal; for us, the return on sales time invested was very high; everyone was happy.

And since the remaining prospects did not want M&A service, that was the end of our venture into beef processing, although—and this is an important point—*it didn't have to be.* We could have kept those contacts alive. While the prospects hadn't felt a need to buy the solution we were offering on this issue, our interaction with them had been cordial, and they saw how well we'd been able to serve one of their peers in the industry. Most of the time, our process would call for building on such a start. It would entail staying in touch with the whole group, with communication about content of interest to them, so as to build relationships that could be extended into future initiatives when they might buy services for other needs—a concept we will, in fact, discuss a little later in this chapter.

In this situation, we chose not to extend. We concluded that for various reasons, the beef processing industry just was not one in which we could fruitfully build sustained high-volume business. Whereas for some types of service firms it might be a perfect fit, a gold mine full of branching veins to be tapped, we had other initiatives under way in markets more suited to us. We decided our time would be better spent focusing on those.

A key message here is as follows: There are different ways of exiting an initiative, and most of them do end, sooner or later. But the strategic four-stage process should never end. You want to push each new initiative for all it can deliver efficiently, while always laying the groundwork for more, to have a succession of waves of revenue on a continuing basis.

BUILDING RELATIONSHIPS WITH CONTENT TOOLS AND EVENTS

In any new initiative, a crucial topic is how to deal with the majority of the clients on your calling lists—the ones who do *not* grant meetings from your initial round of calls.

Suppose that a salesperson or a team makes 100 calls in a given time period and that many are cold calls. Out of the 100, let us assume that only 30 result in actually connecting to a client for a meaningful phone conversation or e-mail exchange. And although some issues are so hot that a very high percentage of the clients reached will want to have meetings promptly, let's say this issue is not one of them: out of the 30 contacts, 5 express strong interest and commit to a meeting.

What do you do with the other 25? Or, for that matter, with the 70 who didn't respond at all to phone messages or e-mail? Some of your best prospects, and much of your prospective volume, may well reside in these two groups. Maybe these clients were not yet "feeling the need" from the rock-ripple impact but they will feel it intensely before long. Maybe they were so preoccupied with other demands that they just weren't ready or able to delegate attention to the new issue that you called about, but eventually they will be.

It is essential to keep on connecting (or trying to connect) with these people in a positive manner. This means not by badgering them but by continuing to give them access to content that is specific to their issues and emerging needs. And there are two basic ways of doing so:

- One is by continued personal contact—typically, e-mails that enclose materials with issue updates that track the progress of the emerging issue or that contain news and analysis of new developments.

- The other is by organizing and staging issue-oriented outreach events that build scale as well as building individual relationships.

The latter could be the roundtable discussions mentioned earlier, physical gatherings to which a salesperson invites perhaps 20 or 30 to 100 clients of the same type from a given geographic area. Or they could be online webinars to which several hundred prospective clients across a wide area are invited to log in. Either way, the event becomes a forum for a presentation by your firm's key professionals, followed by participation and exchange among the clients.

Persistence is essential. Once a target list of clients has been identified, the sales team has to keep developing and sending out e-mails regularly, and staging events regularly, for several reasons. One is the power of repeated impressions. No advertisers would produce only a single print ad or TV commercial and run it just once; they all know the value of "frequency" in creating top-of-mind awareness.

Another reason is that the messages you are sending can actually prompt sales. They are not merely image ads for things that would be nice to buy; they contain information about pressing issues and needs. When well-conceived, each of a series of e-mails or events actually teaches the clients something more about an issue or presents new insights into the issue. And you never know which one might make the connection that makes the difference for a given client, moving the process across the goal line to the point where the person decides "I'd better do something about this" and picks up the phone to call you.

What *we* know is that our e-mails get responses, many of them at a surprisingly high rate. This happens even though they are not written as strident calls to action. Each one simply presents the content we are delivering, usually with the highlights in the body of the e-mail and the meat of the information in an attached file. The cover e-mail ends with, at most, an oblique action message such as "I look forward to discussing this and other issues with you" or, after giving the highlights, something as simple as "Interested?"

Such a one-word closing is highly informal and would be used, of course, only if the sender already has an appropriate relationship with the client. That brings us to the final reason for persistent communication about content. It is done to maintain relationships—and to maintain them on a distinctive basis that differentiates you. It says again and again that you are a guru, a constant provider of fresh insights, someone who can be counted on to think strategically *for the client*.

If you let communication lapse, that standing begins to erode. Then you slide back into a commoditized vendor-buyer relationship, which is a position that you and your salespeople never want to be selling from. You will be much more successful selling within the transformed environment, where you are the client's trusted business resource and a personal asset as well.

SELLING TO BOTH SIDES OF THE CLIENT

How does one become a client's personal asset? In the same sort of way that IBM once did, in the days when the firm's dominance of the corporate computing market used to be explained by the saying "Nobody ever got fired for buying from IBM."

This was often intended as a snide remark, meaning that IBM's equipment was so widely used that it was a safe choice, easy to justify. But

IBM did not begin as the market leader in computing. The firm got there by bringing the market consistent, useful innovations. Early computers were not only much less powerful than later models, they were temperamental, hard to use, and quick to fail. Time and again IBM was first with the improvements that raised performance while also reducing the hassle.

During that period, of course, it was unlikely that any buyers in client companies would be fired for going with IBM. They were likely to look good, win gratitude, and be promoted. Furthermore, having an IBM connection was a route to success for many start-up companies. Intel, Microsoft, Seagate, and SAP all grew into major players in computing by being strategic partners with IBM. These were relationships that helped IBM bring out key innovations—and made fortunes for all concerned, including, naturally, the founders of the start-ups.

So IBM thrived, in no small part, because a lot of people learned that a relationship with IBM had a double benefit. It was good for their companies and good for themselves.

And that is the kind of relationship that you offer to your clients when you consistently bring them news and insights about issues that affect their companies. Not only are you providing information that could help the company deal with a threat or seize an opportunity; you are enabling your contact to look good. That person is the one within his or her company who, in turn, gets to alert others in the organization to emerging issues, after which either of two things may happen:

- If the issue is immediately urgent—and if responding to it saves the company a lot of grief or turns into a big win—your contact becomes the hero who raised the alert.

- Even if high drama does not ensue right away, continued communication has its effect. Your contact starts to be seen as somebody who is well wired, who always seems to have an inside track on new developments.

This is a powerful motivation for the person to be inclined in your favor. Some of your client contacts may be midlevel executives, department heads or the equivalent, who are looking to move up in their careers. Anything that enhances their standing will be appreciated. Other contacts may be members of a senior management team who like to have their viewpoints heard at the table, and they, too, will be appreciative. Just from a psychological standpoint, everyone enjoys having access to unique knowledge. We all enjoy the heads turning and eyes opening attentively when we share such knowledge.

From experience with our own client contacts over the years, we can tell you surely: when you use this communication approach, you are winning friends and influencing sales.

In most client organizations, the contacts you develop will not have sole buying authority on major opportunities. You have to count on them to be your internal champions. Think of how much more effective they can be, in moving a buying decision toward your firm, when you have armed them with hard data and issue analysis that they've been circulating and using to bring others into the loop. You have a credible, committed set of allies within the company. And when they change companies, they have a sound basis for bringing you along.

Bottom line: All clients have twin sets of concerns. They care about their companies, and they care about their careers. They care *passionately* about their careers. When you are able to help them on that front while also addressing their companies' needs, you have the basis of an extremely strong relationship.

Regular communication about valuable content does both. There will be other opportunities to do so as well. Watch for them.

ROUNDTABLES AND OTHER "SCALE" OUTREACH EVENTS

Waves of e-mails (and, for long campaigns, marketing newsletters) are individual communication tools. They are commonly thought of as bulk or mass media, since they go out to multiple clients, but look at it from the clients' perspective. Each is received and read by one client at a time, separately.

We thus complement these with true "scale" events, which bring together groups of clients for interaction about issues of mutual interest. The most common are roundtable discussions, involving anywhere from a couple of dozen to as many as 100 clients from the same target group.

For us, people from banks and financial firms are frequent invitees, since we do a lot of business in the financial industry. We also frequently have legal roundtables because we often partner with law firms in our initiatives. And given that we have a long-running initiative on data breach—a threat that affects nearly every industry—we stage periodic data breach roundtables for executives and others involved in response to breaches.

You would slant your roundtables to *industries or functional areas* in which you have, or expect to have, *either an ongoing major initiative or multiple initiatives over time*. Your target groups could be health care providers, fashion-industry firms, defense contractors or heads of physical plant — it doesn't matter. You can also have virtual group events such as webinars or videoconferences in addition to, or in lieu of, physical roundtables: that doesn't matter either. The purposes would be the same and the dynamics very similar. We will use roundtables as the example throughout because we recommend them strongly.

These events have several functions:

- They allow you to interact with many clients of the same type at once, face to face in real time. There is scale efficiency in this—you are building top-of-mind awareness one to many—and it enables a style of personal interaction that is memorable and distinctive.

- Done regularly, the roundtables build your brand. They become true events that people look forward to, and since they deal with important and relevant issues, they reinforce your guru status within the target group. Some of our roundtables have been used by clients to meet their continuing professional education requirements.

- The roundtables speak to both sides of the client. Clients come on behalf of their companies and also to advance their careers. For example, people from the client firms are usually asked to serve as panel members or guest presenters on the topic of the day. To someone who is an executive or professional on the way up, this is a great opportunity. It is a chance to represent the company in public, to make a strong impression in front of peers, and—since few people stay with one firm forever—a chance to be noticed by a roomful of potential employers.

- Roundtables are opportunities for your firm to get feedback on marketplace issues and to build relationships with potential buyers in a business-oriented but non-sales-pressured setting.

- Finally, roundtables reinforce the community concept that we will talk about in the next section of this chapter. By hosting an event for a professional community, you establish yourself as a member of that community.

The specifics of how to plan and stage a roundtable could fill a small book of their own, but many are standard event-planning details. Here are some key strategic and procedural highlights of how we do it.

Each person on the sales team is responsible for organizing two roundtables (or equivalent outreach events) per year. They can be related to the same initiative or different ones. What's important is for the salesperson to take ownership. Each one is building his or her own sets of client relationships, and therefore he or she must be in charge of the inviting and act as the host.

We also want each person on the team to own the strategic process and the content of each initiative. Therefore, they choose the topics of the roundtables and the speakers—typically, for each event, a group of several speakers or panelists, who come both from our firm and client firms. Our firm provides total logistical support for the roundtables: we want the sales-people focused on relationships and content, not on wrangling with venues and menus.

Choosing topics can be a bit of an art form in itself. There will be a roomful of clients from different firms, many of whom are competitors. You have to stay away from topics such as "how to beat the pants off of every-body else on Issue X," and with any subject, you cannot expect open discus-sion of aspects that would involve revealing confidential information. But just about any issue has plenty of important aspects that clients are mutually concerned or curious about and eager to learn and share about.

We've had successful roundtables on topics such as setting up regula-tory compliance programs and dealing with internal whistleblower issues in investigations. To speak to the clients' career side, we have even had career-oriented roundtables on topics totally unrelated to our sales initiatives, such as negotiating compensation packages.

Altogether, our firm has roundtables for major markets every month or two. Most are luncheons or dinners, with speakers followed by open exchange. We've had big ones, to generate a lot of buzz and awareness; and we have had small ones with as few as eight high-profile executives of client firms to home in on top-level content and relationships.

There are a couple of things we do not do. We do not undercut the credibility of the events by using them as pretexts to present sales pitches, and we don't try to make them elaborate affairs, loaded down with special effects or trappings irrelevant to the business at hand. A good topic with the right speakers for the right guests are all you need—which leads to a general point that applies to everything said here.

KEEP IT SIMPLE

The events are important, and so are the communications you send. Don't overcomplicate them.

If you discover a new development that clients ought to know about, not everything needs to be turned into a formal white paper. Be sure you have the facts and figures right, then put them into a readily shareable form and get it out there fast.

This is the information age. Selling comes from relationships. Use information to build relationships.

EXTENDING RELATIONSHIPS INTO OTHER INITIATIVES

Practically everything that will go into the deployment of any given initiative has now been covered. Standard sales procedures such as diligent tracking of results still apply; you either know how to do those things or can learn them from other sources.

Soon you will have multiple initiatives deployed at once. There is not much more to say about what you need to do in that regard, either. Not much is done differently, aside from the fact that you and your salespeople will have to manage your attention to switch between tasks, which is also standard personnel- and team-management stuff.

The big difference will be in the results. You should have a lot more of them to keep track of—a lot more sales to put up on the board. And they will come in a more consistent, concentrated manner.

THE MULTIPLIER EFFECT AND THE SMALL-WORLD EFFECT

The real multiplier effect of the four-stage process begins to kick in when you have multiple initiatives deployed. For one thing, they are not all at the same stage of progress in the field. A new one has just been launched while the previous one is ramping up and starting to generate sales. Others are at their peak, while the oldest are tailing off. Therefore, you have an ongoing flow of volume sales. Each new initiative that you bring online is not a make-or-break affair; it is one that can *add* to the volume and create growth.

And there is a second benefit. As noted earlier, the relationships that you and your sales force build in each initiative are not necessarily exclusive to it. At least some of your initiatives will be targeted to the same industries, even to the same sets of clients within those industries. This has very often been the case for us. For instance, we targeted financial institutions when we detected the rock-ripple event that became the credit crisis. Then, a couple of years later, when we saw ripples begin to spread from Chinese reverse merger issues, our targets again included financial institutions.

For that second initiative, we already had a number of relationships established. Even if the clients had not bought credit-crisis services, they knew us. They appreciated the fact that we were able to provide meaningful hard information. They had begun to regard us as *gurus* on matters affecting their industry. Approaching them became easier the next time around, and it also has served to reinforce the relationship, laying the groundwork for *future* initiatives and sales.

As you move from serving one wave of need into others, you can create similar spillover effects in the industries that you sell into. The potential connections are there, waiting to be made. You just have to find them.

Out of such effects, areas of specialization will begin to emerge naturally. The better you know the clients in a given industry sector, the more you will pay attention to it, and the more likely you are to spot rock-ripple events which affect it. Your knowledge base builds, and so does your credibility and level of acceptance.

Eventually, you and your salespeople become *trusted members of the communities* to which various groups of clients belong. Any client industry is really a community or a set of communities. Banks, electric utilities, private schools in the Midwest, professional sports teams: name any market or industry sector that might possibly include clients for your firm's services. It will contain a large but finite number of firms or entities. And, whatever the number, there really is a small-world effect. Senior executives and professionals migrate between firms within the community. They attend the same conferences; they have common concerns; they know each other.

And once you reach the stage where enough of them know you, *through relationships built on the exchange of useful content,* you are a member of the club—a respected and knowledgeable guest member. That is, again, a much more powerful position to sell from than "Let me tell you about our firm. . . ."

INDIRECT SALES: THE ULTIMATE PAYOFF

Recently, one member of our team landed what might turn out to be the largest single sale he has made thus far. I say "landed" because it simply landed in his lap with no sales pitch whatsoever on his part.

He had taken a lawyer to lunch. It wasn't a schmoozing, let's-get-to-know-each-other lunch, but rather a purposeful one. Our team member already knew this attorney, from repeated contact about strategic initiatives on which our firm and his law firm either had partnered or had looked into partnering. Now he wanted to introduce the attorney to a person in a related line of business. This bit of matchmaking went well; it appeared that the two parties could form a useful connection going forward.

Then, in the cab coming back from lunch, the attorney turned to our colleague and said, "Oh, by the way. I wonder if you could help us with something," and proceeded to hand him a very significant opportunity. It seemed the attorney's law firm had the inside track on a major piece of long-dated new business. To help secure the job and perform the work, the services of a firm like ours were needed. Rather than ask for formal presentations from a cast of contenders, the attorney had suggested—and the senior people at his law firm had readily agreed—that our firm should be brought in straightaway.

Our sales executive had no prior knowledge of the need, since it had been kept confidential to that point. All that was left to do at that point was to say yes.

This sort of thing has happened to us more than once—many more times than once. And when it happens, it feels *effortless*. The phones are ringing with inbound calls from clients and strategic partners, through no (additional!) work at all. But, of course, never does it truly happen out of nowhere. These indirect sales, which may appear to occur so serendipitously, are in fact part of the payoff for all of the preparation and diligence that go into executing the four-stage process.

They are also part of the payoff for keeping one's focus where it belongs: always on the needs of the people in the marketplace. Nobody has ever brought us into a deal or called us to deliver a premade sale because we wined and dined them or played golf or poker with them. If you were to try that old approach to relationship selling, you would soon learn two things: (1) most clients today do not have time for it, and (2) even when and if you manage to forge a relationship on such a basis, it is a relationship that puts you on a subservient footing. You are transparently trying to curry favor with the client. You are buying his affection and hoping to keep it, whereas by bringing him useful information and insights, in the approach that we have been advocating, you are earning his respect and building professional trust.

To reiterate once again: This four-stage process transforms the act of selling. You are creating value for the client in the course of each encounter, and thereby putting yourself on a different standing entirely. Instead of saying "Please let us work for you," you are placing yourself on a collegial, collaborative basis with the client, which implicitly says: *Of course we can work together. We already are.*

CHAPTER 12

Hunting or Farming? It's Both: An Approach for New and Existing Clients

Before moving on to the end of this book—and to wherever it may take you—some final notes are in order about client relationships and selling styles. We'd like to address a line of thinking that is common in the world of professional sales. This thinking, too, is something that would change when you adopt the rock-ripple approach. So let us look at how the subject is typically thought about, then see how things play out in a rock-ripple selling environment.

There are two sources of future business: new clients and repeating or expanded sales to existing clients. And, clearly, there are differences in how you need to go after the two. You don't talk to a stranger the way you would to someone you know. Forming a new relationship isn't the same as sustaining and growing a relationship—it's sort of like the difference between dating and being married, and so forth.

To an extent, the two kinds of selling call for different skills. Some believe they are best done by different kinds of salespeople. Thus, some sales managers even divide the sales force accordingly, recruiting and deploying people as either hunters or farmers.

In places where the effort is organized that way,

- Hunters are given the task of pursuing new and cold clients. Often put in a group called the new business team or some such, they're the people believed to be really good at making cold calls and getting a foot in the door.

■ Farmers usually are assigned to large or high-potential existing accounts—key accounts, to use a common term. Their job is to deepen and widen the firm's relationships with these clients. Like good farmers, they are expected to tend the key accounts with loving care, keeping the fields free of scavengers (i.e., competitors) and harvesting the fruits in ever-increasing abundance.

The perceived difference is so great that people come to think of themselves in these terms, figuring they have to be *one or the other*. When we interview candidates for a position on our sales team, we like to ask them if they are hunters or farmers. Inevitably, the person will say, "I'm a hunter!" After all, that's the tougher and more glamorous role, isn't it? The hunters are the ones who go out into the wild and bring it home. They don't pray for rain, they make it. They can create business where none existed before!

Certainly, we like candidates who express confidence and energy. We also prefer people who are willing to try something new, since they will have to learn a new way of selling when they join our team.

But, in fact, within the framework of this new way, we do not categorize people as either new-client hunters or key-account farmers. Each person plays what you might call a hybrid role, doing both and having the flexibility to do one or the other as circumstances require. The reasons, briefly, are as follows:

■ Both new and existing clients are critical to the business. In contrast to the individuals who self-identify as hunters, there are professional service firms that tend to lean the other way, emphasizing strategies to get the most from existing accounts. But sales growth is not an either/or game. A farming-style, account-centric strategy has its risks, challenges, and limitations, just as hunting new clients does.

Optimum results come when both avenues are pursued with vigor. And the rock-ripple approach is designed to do this in an *integrated* fashion.

■ The four-stage rock-ripple process is built around initiatives. These sales initiatives, in turn, are built around events in the marketplace—not around whether you know the clients. In a given market sector, a major rock-ripple event will usually create urgent needs for new and existing clients alike. Therefore, the process is aimed at drawing business from both.

Approaches and tactics will differ somewhat, depending on whether the client is existing or new. But, basically, you are building relationships (and eventually winning sales) in the same way: *by delivering timely and useful content about issues that matter to the client.*

- Finally, it's necessary for each individual on a rock-ripple team to work with both new and existing clients for a couple of reasons. If you are the only person taking a particular initiative to market, obviously you will have to sell to both. And even if not, we've found it is vital for each person to "own" the initiative, which means owning all aspects of it.

  Besides, nobody knows which new clients will become tomorrow's key accounts. If you are the one who brings in such an account—and you have done it by building guru status within the client company on the basis of your ability to provide useful information—shouldn't you then continue serving that client as a faithful good shepherd, or farmer, in order to extend and grow the relationship?

  We think so. Of course, adjustments and additions to the team for that client may be needed when an account grows really big, but rarely is it a good idea to change gurus in midstream.

Now let's consider all of the preceding factors in a bit more real-life detail to get a firmer grip on what works best and why.

THE DOWNSIDES OF ACCOUNT-CENTRIC FARMING (AND WHY ROCK-RIPPLE IS SUPERIOR)

"The best customers are the ones you already have." So the old adage says, and in many respects it is true, especially when the client company is a large one. Some years ago, before we joined the firm we are with now, one of our key accounts was a Fortune 50 multinational. Not only is a company of that caliber very large; it presents many points of opportunity for sales growth.

Suppose your firm begins by doing some projects for the executive staff at corporate. Naturally, you'll want to leverage your contacts to start pursuing work in the divisions—of which there are many. If all goes well, you could make nice numbers just by being passed from one part of this company to the next.

But not many client companies are so large and diverse. And all does not always go well.

Here are a few things that can go wrong with a key account:

- A person who is a key relationship leaves.

- A project for the client doesn't work out—perhaps through no fault of your firm, but you will wear the black mark.

- Your firm has done a fine job, but the client just wants to try other firms in order to bring in fresh ideas or different viewpoints. (In our trade, this is called "consultant fatigue" on the part of the client.)

- The client company's own fortunes take a turn for the worse.

- The client is acquired, and suddenly it's a new ball game for everyone involved.

- The client begins squeezing your firm to reduce costs and the assignments cease to be attractive.

Using the rock-ripple approach can help to avoid consultant fatigue, since you are constantly bringing fresh insights to the table, plus in many instances new service packages innovated expressly for an emerging need. However, the other items are beyond your control no matter what selling strategy you use. Not long ago we experienced a cost squeeze from one of our key accounts. The client company had been a growing and regular source of business for us.

This was a valued client, a company full of good people to work with, and our firm was not inclined to walk away from the account. What happened here though is not uncommon, and it can have a pernicious effect. Suddenly, your "key" account becomes one that is actually worth less than the others because your firm is doing a substantial part of its business at eroded margins, which isn't at all what "growth" means. Do you really want to "grow" that account? For some service firms, this can eventually force a hard decision. And again, it is just one of many eventualities that can erode the value of a prized account, regardless of how you sell or how well your firm performs.

Earlier in the book, we emphasized that rock-ripple waves of business have finite life cycles. *Client relationships also have finite life cycles.* If you are lucky, a key account will yield a high and/or growing volume of sales for years to come. But many, perhaps most, will not. There are just too many potential pitfalls. More typically, the yield from a key account will wax and wane in waves of its own (especially if the nature of your firm's service is episodic rather than ongoing), and sooner or later, whether gradually or suddenly, revenue from the account may tail off to the point where it is no longer "key" to your business at all.

What does *not* work well is to ride and flog an account until you hear the large lady singing that curtain time is near, and only then start looking for a new client to replace what the old one provided. That will practically consign you to a boom-and-bust revenue stream.

What works is to follow the rock-ripple four-stage process in the manner recommended. If you focus on what's happening in the market that could affect *large numbers* of clients, be they existing or new, you will be regularly launching initiatives that nurture today's accounts while also bringing the next generation online. There may still be peaks and dips in revenue but the peaks will be higher, the dips not severe, and the overall ride trending upward much more smoothly.

Moreover, in no way does the rock-ripple approach "water down" the service you can give to existing key accounts. Quite the contrary. It should enable you to serve them better than ever. Let us illustrate.

Recently, we made a swing to catch up with various existing and prospective clients over eight meetings that had been booked within an efficient time span of a couple of days. They consisted of six daytime business meetings, one business lunch, and only one dinner engagement. That fact alone underscores two points we've been making throughout the book. First, most clients today do not have time for after-hours socializing; and second, the rock-ripple strategy generates *content* sufficiently compelling that clients chose to take time during the workday to hear about it.

Because, of course, compelling content was the payload we packed for the voyage. The clients to be visited were all in the same industry: finance. Thus, with some variations in what was important to whom, they all had the same intense interest in certain rock-ripple events that we had been tracking. Let us repeat, stating this part explicitly: *The existing key accounts wanted to hear the news and insights we were prepared to share with them.* They found *value* in it. They were extremely well served.

Better yet, there were efficiencies gained for us at every step. Just as promised in this book, the effort we had put into studying rock-ripple phenomena paid off in serious meetings with multiple clients. Then, during the course of those meetings, it was possible to adjust and hone a set of more or less "standard pitches" in seeing how particular points resonated with one client or another. The overall effect was not at all that of a cookie-cutter approach. What you have here is a truly client-centered approach that allows you to work efficiently.

And if you persist in the process, as we have, we think you stand a good chance of seeing what we have seen: business from key accounts and newer accounts that adds up to a highly productive rate of return on time and expenses.

EFFICIENCIES ON THE HUNTING SIDE

Now for more good news. This applies to the hunters in the audience, as well as to farmers who are being called upon to go hunting and wonder if they can do it. Anyone who hunts in real life, with a rifle, will tell you that the hard part isn't shooting the deer. More often, it is finding the deer. Vast numbers of them are out there in deer country. But so are vast numbers of hunters, in deer season, and the deer grow wary of those who enter their turf telegraphing their own needs and intentions. One might spend a long time waiting for a prime prospect to come within range.

The first trick in selling to new clients is to identify likely prospects. And that is precisely what the four-stage process does for you. It identifies, evaluates, and refines lists of *specific* companies that will need *particular* services, before you take that crucial and (for some people) fearful step of reaching for the phone to make a cold call.

There is also a second trick, which is having something to offer that can pique the client's interest in starting a relationship with you. The hunting metaphor actually fails here because clients are not prey. Whereas no deer wants to be shot, clients want and need vital services. So it really makes more sense to think of the whole task in another way. You are not out to hunt new clients; you are out to feed them.

As long as you can reach the right person, and can lead off with an item of direct interest, the client has no reason to avoid you even if you come as a stranger. And the four-stage process equips you to navigate this step with a better-than-average batting average.

Then it makes the sales meeting easier in a variety of ways, which can be very helpful if you are not an experienced salesperson, as there are not quite so many little twists and techniques to learn. For instance, in sellers' jargon, one of the classic face-to-face techniques is knowing when and how to "flip to the sale." It refers to the pivotal moment when you have gone through the preliminary stages of a sales call—which, with a new prospect, can range from introductions and a bit of small talk to speaking about the client's need (which includes surfacing and elevating the need)—and now it is time to actually sell the guy something.

With the rock-ripple approach, this isn't such a big deal. Usually, there is not any golden moment at which flipping should occur. In fact, if you have opened the relationship by speaking of emerging needs the client is likely to have, and are now proceeding to inform the client further about those needs while answering questions that may come up, flipping to the sale usually becomes a nonissue. You don't have to worry about it or try to do it. *It happens of its own accord.*

This apparent miracle transpires because clients are pretty smart. They know that you would like to sell a service, and that you wouldn't be talking about specific emerging needs unless your firm had services to meet them. Therefore, they are capable of putting the pieces together—or, more accurately, the pieces come together naturally as you and the client delve deeper into *what the client will need.*

So, to sum up, you've just had a more explicit explanation of what we mean when we say that this is a more natural way to sell. The rock-ripple four-stage process eases your path and increases your chances at every step of the task of hunting new clients. You don't need to specialize in becoming a mighty hunter.

Nor do you (or anyone on your team) need to devote yourself to farming key accounts, only to discover, as so many real farmers have discovered, that your precious crop is highly susceptible to unlucky changes in the weather.

Instead, you learn a strategy that puts you at the head of the class with both kinds of clients at once.

WHERE THE DIFFERENCES COME IN

We've mentioned that there are some differences in how one deals with new and existing clients, even within the framework of the rock-ripple approach. The book has addressed them already, but we will reiterate them briefly here.

Of course, one must practice the personal niceties, such as not speaking (or e-mailing!) in a highly informal tone to clients with whom one is not on familiar terms. New prospects should be addressed in a more dignified manner, but not with a long wind-up before delivering the goods, either. Speak gracefully and professionally and get to the point, which is the content relevant to the client.

Perhaps you didn't need to hear any of that. You probably know how to relate to your fellow humans. What may be less obvious is an important strategic distinction.

As noted earlier, when testing and deploying an initiative, we normally try it first with existing clients. Does this imperil sensitive key-account relationships? Not in the least, as long as a key guideline is observed. Early testing shouldn't be done with clients who expect a finished, polished presentation. If you do it with existing clients (and/or strategic partners) who are open to chewing over new ideas that might still be rough around the edges, it becomes a win all around.

These clients appreciate the courtesy of being first to hear the latest insights. If they deem it sufficiently urgent and compelling, they may be among the first to buy in. If they have questions or doubts about the initiative, they'll give you feedback that helps to sharpen it. Either way, you emerge with an initiative honed for optimum rollout to new clients—with whom first impressions are critical—and to those other accounts with which every impression is critical.

The overall deployment process thus becomes two-pronged. Indeed, it becomes *progressively* two-pronged, such that it multiplies in impact, as shown in Figure 12.1.

Starting from the left of the figure:

- You begin by rolling out to existing relationships, then (slightly later) to new relationships.

- And each of these thrusts may include two types of targets: client companies plus strategic partners who join you in bringing the initiative to market and in doing the resulting work. These partners could be law firms, banks, public relations firms or insurance firms, professional associations, even product providers—any type of firm that has connections to the businesses you're trying to sell to.

- Then, to the right of the figure, the two branches of each thrust branch out further. You have direct one-to-one outreach to specific clients, as well as one-to-many outreaches such as the roundtable conferences and marketing campaigns that we have discussed.

Considering that every single touch point will be touched repeatedly, with ongoing updates and new content regarding the issue(s) at the center of the initiative, and that you are delivering your content through multiple channels (your own plus your strategic partners' channels), both to existing

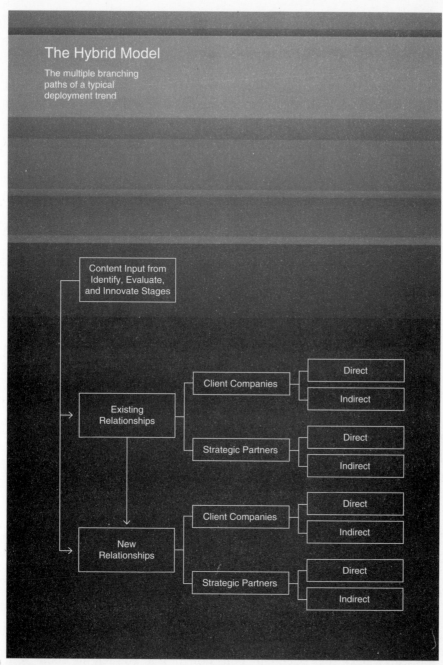

FIGURE 12.1   The Hybrid Mode: The Multiple Branching Paths of a Typical Deployment

clients and to well-targeted lists of potential new clients, it all comes out to a lot of touches. And they are not annoying touches repeated purely for the sake of staying in the client's face: they are content-rich touches that the client will look forward to, and will keep you top-of-mind.

You are able to perform all this efficiently because you have industrialized the selling process, and you can expect returns that multiply to a still greater extent because you will be getting indirect sales, too. Let's consider those for a minute because they bring home an important point.

INDIRECT SALES: THE BIG DIFFERENCE

Indirect sales are ones that you didn't specifically aim to get when you launched the initiative. You set out to sell a well-honed A-list of services, targeted to particular needs of particular clients. Some will buy the A offering, some will not. But, in the process, you learn that a number of the companies also have needs B, C, or D that your firm can meet, which leads to additional sales. This could happen right away or later; it can happen with both new and existing clients; and however it happens, here is the point.

Typically, you learn about these other needs when *the clients come right out and tell you about them*. No fancy cross-selling required. That has been our experience repeatedly. And as noted earlier, the indirect sales typically equal, or exceed, the direct. How is this possible?

It is possible because of the kind of relationships you build with this approach. Even with new clients, you earn *credibility and trust* by bringing them useful content and insights and by following up with more. In the jargon we've been using, you have built (or with key accounts, reinforced) guru status. In plain human terms, you have earned a special standing in the clients' eyes. *You've earned the right to have them open up to you* about their situations because they are confident that you can help them and they would *like* you to help them.

Now think about what this means compared to the old-school way of selling. Every time you have one of these encounters in which a client opens up to you about needs you could serve, you are having the kind of meeting that has long been the goal of sellers everywhere, and which has become nearly impossible to get by conventional means. It's the pain-point meeting, the kind that in the old-school approach you might have called and asked for, with a pitch that essentially boils down to "If you tell me about your needs and pain points, I'll show you how we can help." Clients today won't rise to that bait. They won't take the meeting because they don't have time for what they know is really a fishing-for-sales meeting.

And yet with the rock-ripple approach, here you are having that kind of meeting—precisely because you didn't go blindly fishing. Instead, you came in with content that matters and kept coming in with more of it, which creates a *business relationship* that makes these meetings happen, unsolicited, again and again.

Not to mention that you'll also get referrals and pass-alongs, which (as described earlier) lead to more new client relationships and further indirect sales.

• • •

To sum up, in Figure 12.1 we saw an industrialized sales initiative unfolding, like clockwork, to reap multiplying returns. At the ground level, none of it really occurs mechanistically. Everything remains grounded in building relationships, one client and one partner at a time. But in stepping back to look at the mechanics of it all, you can see the accumulating impact that this selling process is capable of bringing to market. It is quite a system to have at one's command.

CHAPTER 13

Where to Go from Here

In the days when *Collier's Encyclopedia* was sold door-to-door, the salespeople were instructed to ask a closing question after the customers had looked through the sample volume. *Collier's* was a very high-quality encyclopedia, and the question was: "Do you like what you see?"

We are not sitting in a room with you to ask such a question, but since you have read this far into the *Selling Professional and Financial Services Handbook*, you probably like what you've seen about the strategic, content-driven approach to selling. The next step is deciding whether to implement it in your own work at your firm. If you are ready, that's what this chapter is about.

You already have a guide to the nuts and bolts of implementation. The preceding chapters on the four-stage process have covered details such as systems to be put in place and procedures to follow. The first time you execute the process—taking an initiative all the way from Identify through Deploy—those chapters will give you the step-by-step specifics.

Our purpose here is to share with you what we've learned about the deeper aspects of implementation. We will describe the mindset and habits involved in this new way of selling. Then we'll get into the basics of bringing others on board with you. The chapter includes sections on implementing the process at three levels: individually (for yourself or a small group), across a sales team, and throughout the firm.

As with the process itself, no deep science is required. Changing how you sell is, however, a significant undertaking. So let's begin the journey with a final boarding call, just to make clear where this jet plane is headed and what you are buying into.

BOARDING CALL: THE DESTINATION, THE TICKET

For us, the ultimate test of the rock-ripple approach began when we brought it with us to the firm where we are currently employed. We had developed, applied, and refined our methods in previous settings; now we were setting out to implement them from scratch across an entire sales team that one of us (Scott) had been hired to manage. We already knew we had a powerful way to go about selling professional services. This was a chance to test how learnable and transferable it really is.

The year before, the sales team had underperformed. None of them knew anything about the concepts you've been learning here, and not all of them caught on right away or bought in wholeheartedly. But over the next six years (up through the time of this writing), the team's performance exceeded annual sales targets each year, often by substantial margins—and keep in mind that the targets were *increasing.*

From start to end of that six-year period, the actual dollar amount of annual sales grew by *more than 500 percent.* This growth was achieved with only a small increase in the size of the sales team.

Furthermore, to use a cliché that is true in this case, the numbers don't tell the whole story. As team members began to assimilate the approach and make it their own, we saw them experiencing both the excitement and the gratification of being more effective, more valued, more in command of their work than they had ever been.

We liked what we were seeing well enough that it prompted us to write this book. Although we cannot promise that your sales will grow at the same rate, we can say the following about what to expect from a well-implemented rock-ripple approach:

> *You are going to adopt a new way of selling that will transform your selling environment and take you to new levels.*
>
> *It will move your client relationships to a higher and different level, positioning you in the role of guru and trusted adviser rather than "person seeking buyers."*
>
> *Since it is a more natural way of selling, it will give you a new comfort level as well.*
>
> *And if you persist in this way, it can take your production and your productivity to increasingly higher levels, perhaps beyond what you thought was achievable.*

Now here are some things that the approach is not. It is not a set of techniques to be applied to your current way of selling to try to tweak performance. Nor is it a menu of methods from which people can do the parts that appeal to them or make sense to them, skipping over parts that may seem unimportant. The approach is not a straitjacket, either. It allows you (in fact requires you) to exercise your individual powers of analysis and creativity to a very high degree, within the framework of the four-stage strategic process—but the framework works only when used as an integrated whole. No step in the process is trivial to the result.

This way of selling is certainly something you can phase into your existing schedule, by marking off and devoting, say, X hours per week to it at first, then ramping up the share of your work time as needed. Just be sure you allot enough time to implement the entire approach, carrying initiatives through every step of the cycle.

Finally, the rock-ripple approach is not for everyone. Salespeople who are happy with meeting their minimum targets may not be sufficiently motivated to change. This is for people who are committed to seeing how far they can go.

Of course, even those who are content with the minimum may start to come around once they see what others are gaining. If nothing else, they will deduce that a given level of sales can be made with less work and hassle, since the approach is designed to raise productivity. Then they might be interested in trying for more.

As leaders of a sales team, we find this type of progress to be especially gratifying. It means that someone is opening up to new possibilities—in sales, in work, in life. And being open to new possibilities is really what stands at the core of the approach.

IT ALWAYS STARTS WITH WHAT'S NEXT

We've talked repeatedly about the importance of the "What's next?" mindset. You could say it is made up of two closely related attitudes: seeking *continuous renewal* and *continuous improvement*.

Continuous renewal means always scanning the horizon for the next wave—the next rock-ripple event, the next emerging issue around which to build a new strategic initiative. It also includes staying on top of the issues that you're currently riding, so you can communicate new developments to clients and thereby keep your relationships fresh and vital (see Figure 13.1).

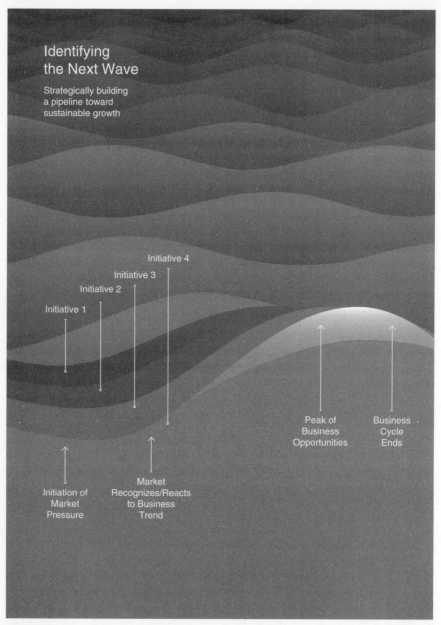

FIGURE 13.1   Identifying the Next Wave: Strategically Building a Pipeline toward Sustainable Growth

Continuous improvement means always looking for ways to raise performance by executing the four-stage process better. Continuous improvement is a concept applied in all sorts of workplaces and there are methods for doing it systematically. We don't use any particular brand-named system; we think the primary ingredient is simply a matter of never resting on your laurels (as in "Selling $100 million is great; now what would it take to get to $125 million?" or "We dodged a bullet and got lucky with this part of the process last time. What can we do to step up the game next time?").

Both continuous renewal and continuous improvement are *cyclical*. You keep repeating the cycle of identifying ideas, refining them, and taking them to market—but with new subject matter each time, and reaching for new levels of insight and excellence each time.

Without getting overly transcendental, one could say that life itself is cyclical in the same senses. It's only truly alive if you keep renewing it.

Moreover, to come back to the business of selling, the rock-ripple approach also has an expansive quality. As you repeat the cycles with increasingly better results, the circle of involvement will tend to expand. More team members and other units within the firm will want to learn the process, which brings us to the sections on implementing individually, for a team, and across a firm.

- Everyone should read the "Individual" section. It's about implementing the approach in your own selling, either alone or as part of a small, cohesive group of people who are committed to learning the four-stage process together.

- The "Team" section is about encouraging and helping others to implement the process. This section assumes that you have the authority to take charge of a teamwide implementation—either as a sales manager, a team leader, or as someone designated to teach the approach, assign tasks, and monitor progress. If your firm is fairly small and you have firm-level authority, what's covered here may be sufficient for implementation throughout the firm.

- The "Firm" section deals with propagating the approach across a professional services firm with more than one sales team and/or operating unit. The assumption here is that you do not have firm-level authority, which means other executives have to be sold on this way of selling.

In each section, we begin by describing what the end state should look like once you have the rock-ripple approach fully up and running. Then we describe what it will typically take to get there.

IMPLEMENTING FOR AN INDIVIDUAL

For yourself or a small group, you will know that you've got things in working order when all of the following hold true:

- The rock-ripple approach has become your primary way of selling, and much of the time it is your only way of selling. You might pursue one-off sales when there is an extraordinary opportunity or a compelling reason to do so, but you don't revert to chasing one-offs as a fallback. Your baseline mode of operation is to build sustained volume and sales growth by working the four-stage process.

- You have multiple initiatives under way, in various stages. Some are deployed and generating sales, while you are moving others toward deployment and laying the groundwork for more.

- Your Identify radar is always on. Whereas at one time you weren't exactly clear on what constitutes a rock-ripple event, you now recognize a range of different types that are liable to affect your clients' businesses. You spot these emerging issues early and often—maybe not every day, but often enough that you sometimes wonder how you ever could have wondered where your next sale was going to come from—and you are quick to evaluate whether and how the ripple effects could create new needs for large numbers of clients.

- The content-driven approach to making sales calls has become second nature. So has the practice of following through on an initiative by sending out issue updates to selected clients.

- You have a growing set of clients who look forward to hearing from you because they value the insights you've given them. A number of them keep showing up on target lists for repeated initiatives. They are probably from the same industry sectors or communities of practice, and some people might say this means that you have developed niches to sell into. It is actually more than that.

- You have become (or are becoming) a familiar, trusted member of these communities. You know increasingly more about their needs and concerns. There are web sites and other sources of information that you scan regularly as part of your Identify and updating exercises; you know people in the communities to whom you can turn for help with evaluating new ideas. In short, you've created an ecosystem within which to sell. And as long as you feed the ecosystem, it keeps feeding you—often with new business that comes in serendipitously, effortlessly.

Now for what it takes to get to this state. In our experience, personal attention to three areas is key:

- First is just making the time to execute all stages of the process diligently. Like you, we have other duties at our firm, some of which are urgent. It is easy to let an initiative slide, especially if you are on a forward-looking step that doesn't demand action today. (For instance, taking time for a periodic formal Identify exercise.) This is not the place for a seminar on time management. Suffice it to say that working the process has to be a priority. It's your daily bread.

- Second, patience is required. You will need to work rapidly and effectively without expecting instant payback. As noted earlier, some initiatives take longer than others to develop. One good indicator of patience: at any given time, you should have some initiatives in the watch-and-wait category. These are the slow-developing ones that can turn out to be big when the rock finally drops or the ripples finally strike.

- The third key is avoiding relapse. Some people are very easily tempted to revert to one-off selling, or to lose confidence in the approach. Any number of forces, both in the external environment and inside one's head, can conspire to undermine a person's efforts. And a long-standing bit of wisdom, which we believe applies here, says there is no use worrying about or trying to fend off all of the negative pressures.

The best way to avoid a relapse is through positive action. *What's next?* Find the next things that have to be done on an initiative and do them. Move the process forward. Build the momentum that builds results.

As you get results, you will move beyond the risk of relapse. You will approach what we call the point of promotion, which has a double meaning. When other people start to notice and appreciate your performance, you might literally get promoted to a higher position in the firm. And you will have earned the credibility to promote the rock-ripple approach. This takes us to the next level of implementation.

IMPLEMENTING ACROSS A TEAM

We can easily tell you what a highly functional rock-ripple team looks like. Whether it is a dedicated sales team, a team of practitioners who sell, or a mixture of both, everything that we said earlier about the earmarks of a good individual implementation still holds true. The only difference is that now these signs are evident in most if not all members of the team.

Each person is identifying new ideas and taking the lead on one or more initiatives. Each is also performing (or is on the road to performing) the additional tasks described in the Deploy section, such as hosting round-table events about emerging issues. Each has created (or is on the road to creating) his or her own personal ecosystem. They all add up to a powerful, synergistic, team ecosystem in which team members are learning from, and leveraging, one another's efforts to sell.

Naturally, some individuals will outperform others, no matter what. But everyone (or nearly everyone) improves and the combined effects produce teamwide results that can be hard to believe.

Getting to this state is not as easy as describing it. Implementing at the team level presents some major differences from individual or small-group implementation. Many team members will not know much about the rock-ripple approach going in, even if they are told to read the book beforehand. In any sample of more than two or three people, individuals may vary widely in terms of how quickly they can grasp the core concepts. And rarely will all the team members be fully committed to learning and practicing the approach.

Much as it is when introducing anything new, there are likely to be skeptics and doubters of every stripe. Objections will range from "This is nonsense," to "I don't need it; I'm already making my numbers," to the frustration of "I just can't get it to work!" The solution that we have found seems to be effective. First, educate. Then see how the chips fall and parse the team into groups, coaching them as we will describe here. We also have a story that illustrates the power of working with a single, willing individual.

Educating the Team

With our new team at our new firm, we began by holding a webinar to explain the approach. This was necessary because some of the team members were on the premises while others were out at various locations. We walked them through the entire four-stage process. We introduced and explained the basic concepts, using examples that are relevant to our firm's business. And we made it clear that use of the rock-ripple approach was going to be the norm.

From there, we began rolling out initiatives for team members to work on, starting with ones for which we, the coauthors, had identified the ideas. Learning by doing is a powerful mode for the learners, but it requires the teachers to focus on multiple things at once. We coached people on specific steps of the process, both individually and in weekly meetings. We reiterated and tried to drive home basic principles—notably the value of the "what's next?" mindset. Plus, of course, we monitored results, keeping in mind that nobody was granting the team a multiyear learning curve: overall performance had to improve.

And before long, we saw team members sorting themselves into three general categories.

Working with A's, B's, and C's

You will probably see the same categories emerging in your team. Speaking very bluntly, they can be described as follows:

- The A's are the people who do more than pick up the process quickly. They are deeply committed to it. You can call them the true believers: eager, enthusiastic, getting results, and loving it.

- The B's are the strivers and seekers. They want to believe, but they may not be learning or getting results as rapidly as the A's—and they are liable to fall off the wagon, deciding the approach just isn't for them.

- The C's are the hardcore skeptics. They are committed to doing it their way. In their own minds, they are the smart ones and it will take a lot to move them.

What we did was to concentrate on working with the A's and the most promising B's, then use those people's successes to enroll the more difficult B's and the C's.

Here is a striking true story of how it played out through one team member.

The Story of a B

Since he was a B, let's call him Ben. He is a hardworking salesperson who had personal reasons, beyond sheer greed, for wanting to raise his earnings. Unfortunately, Ben seemed to be largely at sea when it came to learning the rock-ripple approach. So we made him one of two B's, both eventually successful, whom we targeted at the same time for a move up to the A bracket.

With Ben's agreement, we gave him a fresh initiative, which we judged he was well suited for. It held promise of being a big one. The deal was that Ben would keep after it, and we would keep coaching and supporting him intensively, until he got it to work. All three necks were on the line: Ben's and ours. And seldom have we seen a person so committed to holding up his end of the bargain.

The emerging issue we handed to Ben was in the mortgage servicing space. To describe it briefly, the rock-ripple event we saw looming was a fallout from the earlier subprime mortgage crisis. More specifically, certain mortgage servicers responsible for collecting monthly payments from borrowers were alleged to have committed errors in the process of foreclosing on homes of defaulting borrowers, among other issues. The federal banking regulators were almost certain to take measures, forcing firms to identify any such errors and also to make corrections going forward. This, we foresaw, would create a variety of needs with which our consulting firm is well qualified to help.

We intended to come to market early and win a large share of the business. Ben was our ball carrier. We coached him clear into the Innovate stage, through all the steps of studying the issue and the markets, preparing target lists, and preparing and refining a talk track. Then we turned him loose to start making calls.

Ben was an absolute bulldog. Over a period of nearly a year (while also doing other things, of course), he obtained a number of client meetings and brought major industry participants to a roundtable on the topic. He was definitely making an impression with clients, but he was not yet making a sale. During that whole period we worked with him to step back, tweak and refine, and try again. We tried several iterations of the calling list alone: perhaps he was aiming too low in the client organizations; perhaps he was aiming too high. We experimented with different versions of the pitch. At our team's periodic sales meetings, Ben had the often difficult task of reporting on progress while not being able to report any revenue from the initiative.

As it turned out, one last piece of the puzzle had to click into place. We had sent Ben to market very early—early enough to lay a lot of groundwork, but too soon to close actual sales. Clients were not yet feeling a proverbial gun to the head, forcing them to act. Then, in 2011, the federal banking regulators issued wide-ranging consent orders requiring affected servicers to identify and remediate the issues. The floodgates opened and there sat Ben, ready to reap the rewards of going to market early.

He had had the chance to test and calibrate precisely how our firm could best serve the suddenly emerging need. Nearly everyone who counted in the client universe regarded our firm as a leader, if not *the* leader, in the field. He knew the issues well, having studied as if his life depended on it.

Within the next year, Ben shot up the charts to the point of being either the team's top-ranked or second-ranked producer. Not only did he have a landmark success to his credit; he had built a strong platform for related initiatives in the future.

And he has dramatically affected the tone of our sales meetings. Now, when Ben steps up to talk about what he has accomplished and how he did it, everyone listens intently. Team members who were highly skeptical of the rock-ripple approach have been moved to reconsider.

Conclusions

The story doesn't really have an ending. For Ben, the sky is the limit. You might read *his* book someday.

For the team, the annual sales volume figure that we once set as a long-range goal—which looked like a real reach at the time—is becoming a milestone we passed a while ago. The question that lies ahead now is whether it would be possible to double the figure. We haven't even told you about Mike, the second B in our focused coaching effort who is making the A list as well, nor about the other B's and the C's who have considerable upside potential they are only starting to recognize.

Most vitally, we have a team learning more each day about continuous renewal and continuous improvement. And people in other parts of our firm have taken notice.

IMPLEMENTING ACROSS A FIRM

The ideal would be to have an entire firm going to market with the content-driven rock-ripple approach. For people to practice this approach effectively, they have to be sold on its benefits rather than ordered to adopt it. So the best way to institute it throughout a firm is gradually and organically, the way that we have been doing.

If you start by *demonstrating* success with individual sellers, gradually a team buys in. Then, as you demonstrate team-level success, gradually the approach can be propagated into other teams or business units, as people step forward who are willing to learn and lead.

Even at a progressive firm like ours there are resistances to be overcome. To begin with, at any given time, a large number of popular new movements, systems, and approaches are sweeping through the management world. How are executives to know that rock-ripple-guru isn't just another fad?

Credibility comes only from results. Thus, the first step must be to build results, within some part of the firm, of such a magnitude that they can neither be ignored nor written off as luck.

Then, once eyes are opened by results, ears are opened, too. People across the firm become more receptive to hearing about other inherent benefits of the rock-ripple approach. Here are four that can help to win converts internally:

- One is the naturalness of the selling approach. No firm today can count on a dedicated sales force to bring home the bacon. At our firm, consultants have to sell; at your firm it may be attorneys or some other practicing professionals who have to sell more, and more effectively, than they have in the past. This content-driven approach lets them sell from their natural strength as content experts.

- Closely related is the fact that the rock-ripple approach does not constrain people's freedom. Professionals are apt to balk at any new system or method that looks as if it will force them into a mold, limiting their ability to exercise their own judgment and creativity. This approach does just the opposite. It liberates them—indeed, calls upon them—to be more creative, more open to new ideas, more strategically in charge of their selling.

- Both for individual sellers and for the firm as a whole, it is a proactive approach aimed at taking leadership on market issues. To people who are weary of just trying to make numbers or tread water, that is a game worth playing.

- Finally, clients like the approach. That is why they buy.

In short, this new way of selling is an idea that grows on people. It grows more and more attractive as more people in the organization learn to use it to produce results.

And, when people want to learn, you will have *the book* that shows them how. We've written the basic explanatory book, the primer on the approach, which is coming to a close here. It is up to you to take the principles and run with them. Make them your own and write the other book—the book of business that grows larger as you learn.

WHAT'S NEXT?

Once again, the story has no ending, only another beginning. Go out and do it. Let us know about your successes. Before long, you might be able to teach us a few things. If so, we'll put them in the next edition. It's your story now.

Appendix A
Books for Further Reading

In this book we have described a new, powerful, and distinctive approach to selling. Why, then, would we suggest that you read somebody else's book? Because it might help you derive maximum value from this one.

Selling Professional and Financial Services Handbook gives you a superior strategic framework. And from there, as with so many things in life, it's all about execution. Getting optimum results will depend not only on how you apply the strategic principles, but on how you exercise your own creativity within this framework—and on the selling "tactics" you use within the context of the overarching strategy. That's where the other books come in. The ones here delve more deeply into tactical aspects of selling to a given client.

For instance, *Selling Professional and Financial Services Handbook* lays out a highly productive way to identify and target clients who will need your services, then goes on to describe (among many other things) a comprehensive set of approaches for obtaining and preparing for meetings with these clients. That is a lot of useful front-end information you won't find elsewhere. But it does not deal much with the particulars of face-to-face selling, assuming, as Chapter 10 says, that "you either have such basic skills, or can learn them from other fine sources."

So here are a few fine sources. We've read them ourselves and have found the authors' ideas useful and enlightening. Typically, these books will pick you up somewhere in the "obtaining and preparing for a meeting" stage, then take you into the particulars. The books have overarching philosophies of their own, but for the most part they're philosophies that are congruent with ours, which is one reason we have singled them out. Not only should you find some good "tactical" advice in these books; it's advice that should fit nicely with the rock-ripple strategy.

- *SPIN Selling* by Neil Rackham (McGraw-Hill, 1988). A classic must-read on how to conduct effective sales discussions and presentations. (One hint:

Ask different kinds of probing questions to fully develop your understanding of the client's need before connecting to your proposed solution.) This book is a longtime favorite of ours and can be of benefit to anyone selling any type of professional service.

- *Selling the Invisible* by Harry Beckwith (Orion Business, 1999). Another early and influential book that deserves to be on everyone's list as a foundational read. The author goes into some detail on how to sell services and what makes it different from selling products. The book underscores the point that in selling a service, you are really selling a relationship.

- *How to Become a Rainmaker* by Jeffrey Fox (Hyperion, 2000). One of the best books on core sales skills, which are applicable to selling any solution or to the execution of any sales strategy. Whether you are new to sales or a seasoned veteran, the book is worth revisiting regularly to ensure that you are deploying a full range of proven tactical skills.

- *Escaping the Price-Driven Sale* by Tom Snyder and Kevin Kearns (McGraw-Hill, 2007). Cowritten by a former CEO of Huthwaite, the sales training company behind SPIN Selling, this book helps sellers differentiate from their competition by noting that clients will pay a premium for insights, analysis, and expertise that they can derive from the sales process. We especially recommend the book for anyone selling to the C-suite.

- *The Challenger Sale* by Matthew Dixon and Brent Adamson (Penguin Books, 2011). The authors present a series of findings about what top solution sellers do to compete successfully. They argue that, among other things, complex sales require a focus on insight, tailoring the message for the customer, and challenging the customer to think differently.

- *What the Customer Wants You to Know* by Ram Charan (Penguin Books, 2007). This last book on our short list, by an eminent business thinker best known as a management (not sales) consultant, should be more widely read than it is. One key point: Rather than going into a sales conversation with the objective of showing how smart your solution is, start with a deep understanding of the client's need, which will allow effective sale of very specific solutions to the client's most pressing problems.

Any or all of the books here, with their good advice on the basic aspects of personal selling, can help you get the most from the rock-ripple strategy. And, of course, the converse is true. No matter how you sell currently, we think *Selling Professional and Financial Services Handbook* can help you make a quantum leap forward.

Appendix B
Strategic Initiative Checklist

The checklist here presents, within a single general outline, all major steps of the four-stage strategic sales process described in this book. It is a slightly modified version of an actual checklist that we, the co-authors, have used and distributed in our firm.

Each of the four stages has key action items listed. Near the end you'll notice that special attention has been paid to follow-through in the Deploy stage.

I. Identify Stage

- Monitor changes and impacts:
  - Global
  - Regulatory
  - Economic
  - Technological
  - Precedent-setting litigation
  - Environmental
  - Social
  - Demographic
- Sources to monitor can include:
  - General news and business news outlets
  - Selected websites
  - Online newsfeeds
  - Clients and strategic partners

- Other personal contacts in industries of interest

- Practitioners, research staff, and other colleagues at your firm

- Look for rock-ripple events: emerging trends or issues that could create urgent needs for large numbers of clients—especially in unexpected or little-discussed ways. These can be the basis for strategic initiatives.

- Scheduling for this stage:

  - For print and online sources: Have a regular (daily) monitoring time, plus periodic reviews.

  - With personal sources: Inquire about new developments whenever possible.

  - In general: Always be on, eyes and ears open to opportunities.

II. Evaluate Stage

- Evaluate each opportunity with *consistent, robust analysis.* Key questions are:

  - Is this trend in fact likely to happen, on any significant scale at all?

  - Is it worth pursuing for your firm?

  - Where and how should you enter (e.g., with what solutions, for which kinds of clients) to get maximum returns from an "industrialized" initiative?

- The goal is to build a *business case* for a strategic initiative or to find that such a case can't be made. Possible outcomes:

  - "Yes, *and* . . ." (The idea is a go, and you now have basic plans for how to go forward.)

  - "No"

  - "Watch and wait"

- Evaluation items include:

  - Basic reality testing: Test your perception of the opportunity with lead practitioners (see below) and/or other trusted sources.

- Is the trend going to be a hot issue? Will it create urgent needs for clients? Will they and other stakeholders recognize and value your active development of an initiative aimed at the trend?

- Does the trend have scale—that is, multiple new business opportunities, each of sufficient size, with the potential to generate significant new revenue?

- Which *identifiable* clients will be affected (and can you identify them)?

- What specific needs will be created, for whom?

- What solutions can you offer?

- Does your firm have optimum solution sets ready to go? If not, can you create them, and what would that take?

- Who are your competitors likely to be?

- How, and how successfully, can you differentiate yourself? (For example, can you go to market early enough to win initial sales and build guru status with the content-driven, rock-ripple selling approach? Can your firm remain a viable and even preferred choice when other competitors enter?)

- What is the opportunity cost of developing this initiative as compared with other uses of your business development resources?

- Identify lead practitioner(s). A lead practitioner is someone in your firm who is expert in delivering the solution, and who is therefore in a prime position to provide input and feedback on the strategic initiative.

- Conduct and conclude the evaluation. Use quantitative methods where needed (e.g., to estimate size and margins on a typical project, or to estimate the cost of gearing up for the initiative), but avoid the trap of using numbers and projections as a substitute for good business judgment.

- Time frame for this stage:

  - Typically, three to five business days.

  - Can be shorter if you reach an early and definitive "No."

  - Can be longer when evaluating a very complex, high-stakes opportunity, or one that moves to the "watch-and-wait" category.

III. Innovate Stage

- Innovate solution offerings, as needed: Coordinate with others in the firm to develop new solution sets, add staff or resources, and so on.

- Prepare launch package for selling team. Package will include:

  - Target list of companies, executives, existing relationships, outside counsel.

  - Summary and background materials on the issue.

  - Sample "Talk Track" for calling (and/or sample emails, elevator pitch).

  - Qualifications of the firm.

  - Tracking sheet.

- Assignments of selling team members to a particular initiative (or to particular clients within the initiative) can be done on the basis of multiple factors, including: geography, capability and experience of various team members, and availability of these team members.

- Prepare marketing campaign, as appropriate:

  - Generate marketing collateral.

  - Identify marketing and speaking opportunities.

- Make plans to generate ongoing top-of-mind tools, which can include new and updated content for selling team to use, periodic marketing newsletters, and so on.

- Distribute launch package materials (often done via e-mail, with materials also posted in a secure electronic team room).

- Arrange for reporting-up requirements; arrange ongoing coordination among selling team, practitioners, and firm leadership.

- Time frame for this stage: typically one to two weeks.

IV. Deploy Stage (Including Follow-up)

- Schedule and conduct launch call, with practitioner(s) and assigned selling team members. Include Q&A and be sure that all are clear on what to do.

- Begin ongoing, in-action coordination among selling team members, practitioners, and firm leadership.

Two Weeks after Launch Date:

- Organize a calling competition to determine who can generate the most client meetings, if initiative has more than one seller assigned.

- Schedule call with selling team to assess progress on newly developed initiative.

- Schedule call with practitioner(s) to provide update.

One Month after Launch Date:

- Pull data from your sales tracking tools, and evaluate.

- Schedule a call with selling team to assess planned activity versus what is being reported.

  1. Identify and address any issues, concerns, and so on.
  2. Share any news on what's working well (including new approaches or talking points that team members have come up with).
  3. Determine action plan on how to continue to move forward.

Following Months after One-Month Assessment:

- Establish a biweekly or monthly call with selling team to ensure there is consistency and accountability for the initiative, and to review results. All team members will report recent activity on this call. Featured team members must demonstrate how they are:

  - Creating scale—Since each initiative presents multiple new business opportunities, the report should show how activity is taking advantage of the full scope of these opportunities.

  - Leading or supporting the firm's efforts on the initiative—through roundtables or webinars, joint ventures with strategic partners, the creation of white papers or research reports for dissemination, and the like.

  - Provide evidence of lead success indicators—for example, numbers of meetings, numbers of proposals, wins/losses.

- Eventually, everyone on the team should organize and lead a roundtable or webinar, and ideally everyone should contribute unique outreach documents.

- Be constantly generating (and using) new top-of-mind tools: updated reports on the trend in question, for dissemination to clients; new marketing materials such as newsletters and white papers, and so on.

- On the basis of sales results, evaluate whether the strategic initiative is still worth pursuing. Decisions may be made at any time to ramp up a given initiative, scale it back, or terminate it.

Strategic Initiative Reporting Structure:

- Monthly reports on each strategic initiative—in spreadsheet form, with details.

- Quarterly report on *all* strategic initiatives that would entail a spreadsheet, with all of the required metrics for each to be provided to team leader in a summary scorecard.

- Regular production of strategic initiative performance data, as required, to assist with information requests from firm leadership.

Benefits of Follow-up Process and Structure:

- Enhanced management of strategic sales initiatives.

- Heightened accountability among the entire selling team.

- Continuous evaluation of what works and what doesn't work, to make better-informed decisions on any given initiative.

Appendix C
Key Concept: ROCK-RIPPLE

Why the Sales Climate Is So Tough . . .
and How a New Strategy Fits In

Client firms today run lean. With tight budgets, they'll only buy true "need-to-have" services. Plus, their key people have tight schedules. They won't take time for standard sales presentations or for old-style, wine-and-dine relationship selling.

What clients *need* today is an extra, expert set of eyes on the horizon. Immersed in daily busy-ness, they're often ill prepared for new threats, demands, or opportunities taking shape at the fringes of their radar. Nor has the "information revolution" been much help. Most clients don't have time or staff to sift and analyze all the information that's available.

The authors of the *Selling Professional and Financial Services Handbook* first realized this in the 1990s, while working at a Big 4 accounting/consulting firm. They decided their own selling time could best be spent in a new way: *by learning to become—literally—the advance scouts and emerging-need advisers to clients, who would then buy services for those needs.*

The result was a selling strategy that has produced high-yield results, over the years, for multiple kinds of professional-service firms they have worked with—including firms in financial services, consulting, and law.

- In their most recent position, they grew revenues of the business development team by more than 500 percent over six years.

- Time and again they've been early to detect, and understand, the implications of critical events or trends. In this way they have sold services related to:

  - The early stages of the credit crisis.

  - Precedent-setting court decisions.

- Compliance with new standards (such as ICD-10/5010 in health care).

- Security threats, such as data breach.

- Marketplace shifts in steel, utilities, and other industries.

No crystal ball is needed to get similar results. It all starts with a simple concept.

WHAT ROCK-RIPPLE MEANS

Disruptive events and trends happen constantly in business. Some are sudden (e.g., natural disasters) but most build gradually: precursor events have been happening for months or years before they converge into a big disruption. Either way, here are the common threads.

Just as a rock dropped in a pond will create ripples across the entire pond, a major disruptive event—a rock-ripple event—can create waves of need across entire client industries. Some ripple effects are obvious and easily predictable, but many are not. Or clients may need help to grasp the full implications.

This is where you, the seller, come in. Using methods described in the *Selling Professional and Financial Services Handbook,* you learn to:

- Scan various information sources—from the Internet to "human intelligence" from your firm's practitioners—for early signs of rock-ripple events.

- Notice ripple effects that are *little understood* at present (e.g., will a rock dropping in Industry A kick up ripples in Industry B? Or do client firms really grasp what they'd have to do to respond to new regulations?).

- Home in on the ripples that would trigger *urgent service needs* for *large numbers* of clients. That's far more powerful than chasing one-off sales.

IF EVERYTHING CHECKS OUT, YOU HAVE THE BASIS FOR A ROCK-RIPPLE SALES INITIATIVE . . .

You make a list of target clients and just offer to share what you've learned. It could be something like: "On issue X, firms like yours are becoming vulnerable to [lawsuits, investigations, new competition, etc.]." Or: "Complying with mandate Y will be trickier than expected," or "A new market window is opening in Z. . . . "

With this strategy, *you don't even need to sell hard*. If you have useful and timely information, many clients will grant meetings to hear it. And many will eventually buy services.

. . . AND FOR WINNING "GURU STATUS"

Moreover, if you keep up the strategy—with ongoing news and analysis of rock-ripple events—you build *client relationships on a new footing*. Clients come to see you as their "guru" on emerging issues. You offer value with every encounter, making you top-of-mind whenever clients need services.

In applying the rock-ripple strategy consistently, the authors have seen a powerful booster effect. About half of their revenues, in a typical initiative, come from "indirect" sales. That is, many clients buy other services *in addition to* (or *instead of*) services for the emerging needs they've been told about.

That is "relationship selling" based on trust and credibility earned. To learn more, see the **Four-Stage Strategic Process** and the **Idea-Starters and Tools**.

Appendix D
The Four-Stage Process

Merely knowing the rock-ripple concept can bring in occasional sales, but it has to be used in a way that goes well beyond standard attempts at trend-spotting.

- The business world is full of future hype and false alarms. If you jump on emerging issues too hastily, you are likely to waste time and money chasing trends that don't play out as expected—or that just don't present the right opportunities for *your* firm.

- Nor does it pay to be late. If you wait until new sales opportunities are blatantly evident, you'll always be climbing on a crowded bandwagon, hard-pressed to differentiate your firm from the rest of the pack.

The goal is consistent, volume sales growth. That requires a systematic process for applying the concept and for building strong sales initiatives around it. The *Selling Professional and Financial Services Handbook* lays out a proven process with four stages:

1. **Identify** rock-ripple events and their likely effects on potential clients. (See **Idea-Starters and Tools** for suggestions on how to begin.)
2. **Evaluate** the opportunity. This is a rigorous process that can tell you both whether and how to pursue a given initiative. (See the **Evaluation Checklist** for guidance here.)
3. **Innovate** the sales initiative. The goal of this stage is to assure that you take your best possible shot, preparing yourself and your team thoroughly. As described in the book, the steps are highly situation-specific. Along with creating scripts and materials for calls on clients, you might work with others in your firm (or with strategic partners) to develop custom service solutions and/or marketing tools.

4. **Deploy** the initiative. Here again the steps are situation-specific, but there are several common threads:

- *Rock-ripple initiatives are not blitzes designed to bring in lots of sales right away.* Most client firms will not buy professional services that quickly, even for urgent needs. Rather, the intent is to get in front of clients, and to stay top-of-mind with them, by continually giving them news, insights, and updates on the issue in question—so that when they are ready to buy, they'll buy from you.

- *All aspects of the initiative, from timing and content to the methods used to approach prospective clients, must be geared to the nature of the opportunity.* For example: In one initiative, the authors had detected a new pattern emerging in government investigations into Medicare claims. This was real news, not widely publicized as yet, and it boded to have impact on a well-defined set of clients in the health care industry (who would need to document that they'd been doing business properly). So a highly targeted and relatively quick-hitting initiative was deployed. It was built around brief e-mails to a list of prime prospects, simply alerting them to the news and offering to discuss the issue in more depth. Numerous clients promptly asked for meetings, leading to multiple sales of related services.

  Another opportunity was nearly the opposite in nature. In the early 2000s, it grew evident that data breach would be a long-running and chronic concern for client firms of all kinds, in every industry. The authors used the systematic four-stage process first to determine what kinds of services their consulting firm could offer most competitively, in relation to this issue. Then they designed a long-running and wide-ranging initiative, complete with marketing materials such as a quarterly "Data Breach Newsletter" that aggregates news and analysis of current trends in the topic. Meanwhile, they kept enriching and refining their selling approaches—for example, by finding strategic partners who could help them gain entrée to clients with pressing needs. All of this led to an ongoing and gradually building series of sales.

- *Monitoring and evaluation of results from a rock-ripple initiative must be qualitative as well as quantitative.* It's not enough just to see if sales team members are making their numbers. Sales meetings are built around questions like "What's next?" and "What can we do better?"—always with an eye to serving the clients better, with guru-like insights and analyses that matter to them.

- Finally: *One must always be identifying new rock-ripple events—and developing new initiatives—while current initiatives are under way.* This helps to avoid the dreaded boom-and-bust cycle, which can take a heavy toll on any professional service firm. New opportunities are always emerging. The goal is to seize the right ones, at the right times, and keep growing.

THE FOUR-STAGE PROCESS IN GRAPHIC TERMS

Figure A.1 shows what a wave of new business from a rock-ripple event looks like. Whether the event makes clients scramble to meet new threats, enter new markets, or comply with new standards, the need for related services will rise and fall roughly as shown in the figure.

As mentioned elsewhere, the duration of the wave can vary greatly. The client need that's triggered might be a one-time need that surfaces, crests, and fades within a couple of years. Or, once the wave has peaked, it could persist at a high level indefinitely. But there will always be a crucial trigger phase and run-up period. It's during these times that you put the four-stage process into action (Figure A.2).

By being early to detect and act, you gain a decided edge over competitors. Notice, too, that numerous other waves are unfolding across the background of the graphic. That's what the business universe always has looked like: new needs are constantly surfacing, while existing needs course through the picture and die off. By constantly *cycling through* the four-stage process—identifying the next waves of need that your firm can serve, and developing new sales initiatives, even as the present ones are in deployment—you gain a cumulative edge and sustained growth.

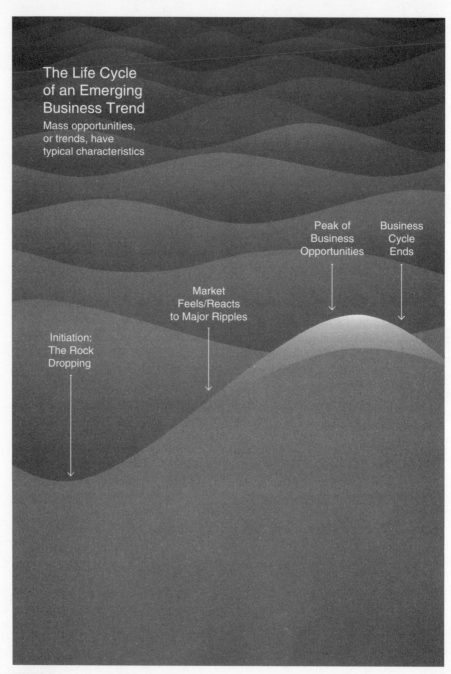

FIGURE A.1

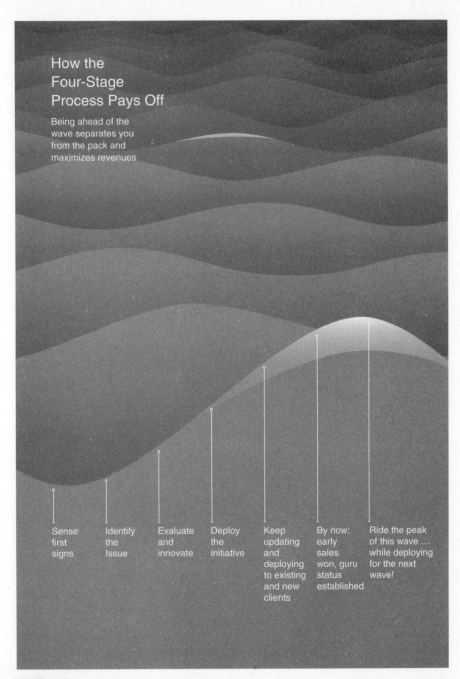

FIGURE A.2

Appendix E
Idea-Starters and Tools

Here are some resources to help you get started with conceiving and developing rock-ripple sales initiatives.

IDENTIFYING ROCK-RIPPLE EVENTS: WHERE TO LOOK FOR NEW SALES OPPORTUNITIES

Opportunities can originate from almost anywhere. The one constant is that new client needs are created—and new sales of services are made—as an outcome of *changes* in the business environment. Just keep in mind that new rocks are always dropping, and they can have far-reaching ripple effects. Whatever the type of services that your firm offers, you might then look for opportunities coming from any or all of these areas:

- *Global events.* Changes in international relations, or in business or political conditions in other countries, can impact anything from national security policy (and thus defense spending) to financial markets to the markets for almost any goods.

- *Changing economic conditions.* And it's important to keep an eye on regional as well as national trends.

- *New legislation or regulatory rulings.* These are obvious game-changers, since they dictate what people can or cannot do, and they also may alter incentive structures (as with changes in tax laws).

- *Technology.* Volumes have been written about the many impacts of technological change.

- *Environmental issues.* These could range from new standards or trends (e.g., in the use of renewable energy) to disputes over practices like shale-gas drilling.

- *Social changes.* When lifestyles or attitudes shift, or when people begin to care about new societal issues, the effects can ripple through the business environment in multiple ways. Spending patterns and buying habits can change; the kinds of laws and public policies that people support can change; and so on.

- *Demographic trends.* The aging of the population and the increase in immigrant population in some regions are examples of trends that can have far-reaching impacts.

- *Precedent-setting litigation.* Court decisions can impact businesses by expanding or limiting their exposure to tort liability, or to antitrust suits or shareholder suits; or by upholding or striking down local laws, and so forth.

The list may seem long and daunting: how could anyone keep track of all these arenas of human activity? But with a little practice, you will learn to home in on changes that could somehow lead to business for *your* firm.

FOOD FOR THOUGHT: EXAMPLES OF REAL ISSUES IDENTIFIED

The authors' firm, Navigant Consulting, Inc., publishes a wealth of online materials about new issues and trends that can impact client needs in many industries. Since the materials are constantly updated with new entries, browsing them may trigger ideas for your firm. Here are links to postings on current issues in:

Financial Services:
www.navigant.com/insights/industry_and_services/financial_services

Health Care:
www.navigant.com/insights/industry_and_services/healthcare

Energy:
www.navigant.com/insights/industry_and_services/energy

Construction:
www.navigant.com/insights/industry_and_services/construction

"Hot Topics" in various industries:
www.navigant.com/insights/hot-topics

EVALUATING OPPORTUNITIES: A CHECKLIST

Stage 2 of the four-stage process—Evaluate—is where you separate the real opportunities from the ones that won't fly. Below is a step-by-step checklist for use with rock-ripple events that you have detected.

All of the following need to be examined, nailing down specifics as much as possible. You may call on your firm's practitioners and other subject-matter experts for help with many of these items.

First, confirm and examine the details of the rock-ripple sequence that you believe you've identified. Begin with the dropping of the rock—the trigger event that will create an urgent or compelling need. (It could be either a single event or a confluence of events or forces.)

- Has this trigger event already happened? (Or is it unfolding now?)

- If not, then when is it likely to?

- Is this inevitable? If not, best estimate of the likelihood?

- And likewise, where and when will the ripples strike, compelling people to take action?

If the compelling need isn't likely to be triggered any time soon, *which you can identify*, then put the idea on to the "watch and wait" track—and keep watching for the trigger event.

The next items are:

> *Who will be impacted by this event? Will there be enough of them to make this an industrial-scale opportunity? And what will they need?*

- As to who will be impacted: the important thing, at this stage, is to be sure you have an *identifiable* group of potential clients *and a means of identifying them and reaching them*. This may sound like an obvious thing to verify, but it is essential. In the next stage, you will be targeting particular firms and people within the firms, to whom to sell. You must know that you'll be able to determine who they are, and how to get to them.

- Will there be enough—in other words, will there be an entire "school of fish" that you can go out to catch? (Or a number of big whales?) As for how many would be enough in a given case, just keep in mind that you will not get them all, and there have to be enough so that with a respectable batting average, the campaign will be worthwhile.

- Finally, as to the services needed: be specific. Exactly how will the ripple affect the clients? Will it put them in a need-to-have, rather than a nice-to-have, situation? *Enumerate and describe* the services they'll need.

- Various clients may need different types or clusters of services, or at different times or on a different scale. If so, divide them into meaningful categories. Some may turn out be your prime prospects, some not.

How do these needs map to your firm?

- What are the services you could offer?

- If they'd be different for different clients, put them into the categories you've created. You may start to find that some map better than others or look more promising.

- If your firm would have to add staff or otherwise gear up, see "Investment needed" below.

What is your differentiator? What will persuade people to buy from you, rather than from somebody else?

Now you get into seeing precisely what can or will distinguish you, and this is also where you get into analyzing both the competition and the clients' buying tendencies. So, again, be as specific as possible, enumerating and describing where needed:

- Will you be early enough to "bring the news" to clients or present it in a new and compelling way, thereby establishing guru status? What will be the nature of your pitch? (You can start generating or at least outlining your sales script here.)

- What are your firm's qualifications for the work?

- Who will be your likely competitors?

- Are any of them onto this trend? And what are they doing? Are they already actively selling—or at least offering services "labeled" to this new need, to try to position them for the wave to come? Are they trying to stake out thought leadership with speeches, white papers, blogs, mailers, whatever?

- Do they have existing relationships with your targeted clients? How will you displace them or preempt them?

What can you learn about the buying tendencies of your likely target clients?

- Do they tend to be early adopters, last-minute rush buyers, or in between?

- What do they tend to look for, in choosing between service providers: comfort level, brand name, low price, leadership, speed of service, and so on? How loyal are they to, or dependent upon, existing service providers?

- What does any of this tell you about how to put together a selling campaign? What are the prospects of high-volume wins?

If you still believe you have a viable selling opportunity, take a closer look at what it will mean for your firm to actually perform the work.

What are the typical sizes of the projects that will result from sales?

Put down the best figures you can for each of the following:

- The approximate dollar value of a project.

- The ranges, if you will be offering different types or clusters of services.

- Your firm's typical margins on this type of work.

What investment and preparation will be needed?

Will you need to add expertise, buy equipment, or take other steps to gear up or to be competitive?

- If so, enumerate and describe what will be required.

- Is it feasible to get, or do, what you need?

- What will be the rough cost?

- If the needs and costs will be different for different groups of clients, categorize them.

The numbers and needs you have projected will give you a picture of the feasibility, profitability, and desirability of the work.

Consider, also, that the future is uncertain:

> *Are there any external factors that could CHANGE anything you have evaluated and projected here?*

If so, enumerate and describe them. And try to project the likelihood of key events turning out (or not turning out) as you expect them to.

Be careful and thorough in assessing risks, but you don't need to try to assign numerical probabilities to them. If you simply list the things that have to be done—or that have to happen—and label the risk level for each as "low," "moderate," or "high," the pattern that emerges will tell you the overall riskiness of going after the opportunity.

Once you have addressed everything listed here, you should have a thorough enough evaluation to reach one of the following decisions:

- "Yes, we're going forward with this, and here are the details . . ."

- No.

- Watch and wait.

About the Companion Website

This book includes a companion website, which can be found at www.wiley.com/go/paczosa (password: peruchini). The companion website contains:

- A video of the co-authors briefly explaining why they developed their strategic sales approach and how it should it be applied.

- Concise (under 1,000 words) primers on the rock-ripple concept and the four-stage strategic process, for use in learning or in presenting these basics to your colleagues.

- A section called "Idea-Starters and Tools," for the critical first two stages of the process. Stage 1—identifying rock-ripple events to serve as ideas for initiatives—is a type of task unfamiliar to most newcomers, so there are two online aids: a recap of the "Where to Look" list from Chapter 4, and a set of links to postings on the website of the co-authors' current firm. These materials, constantly updated and refreshed, are articles about actual disruptive events in various client industries. And for Stage 2: Evaluate, there is a step-by-step Evaluation Checklist drawn from Chapter 7 of the book.

The primers and the Idea-Starters and Tools can also be found in the appendixes of this book.

About the Authors

Scott Paczosa is a managing director at Navigant Consulting, Inc. In addition to leading the firm's business development team, Scott is global leader of strategic initiatives, focused on identifying emerging risks and developing strategic responses. During his 20-plus years in the market, he has been a partner or managing director with prominent firms, such as Ernst & Young LLP, LECG Corporation, and Mesirow Financial.

Throughout his career, Scott has coordinated a wide array of services to clients ranging from Fortune 10 corporations to law firms, and across numerous industries including banking, health care, energy, finance, insurance, security, steel, and transportation. Services have included investigative and litigation services, expert witness testimony, restructuring, valuation, strategy, M&A, due diligence, compliance, and innovative risk reduction.

Chuck Peruchini is a managing director of business development at Navigant Consulting. Prior to his tenure with Navigant, Chuck was national head of business development for Duff & Phelps Corporation and a member of Ernst & Young's business development team. (The authors met and worked together at Ernst & Young.)

Chuck is focused on developing relationships with lawyers and C-suite executives for the purpose of providing insights and solutions to issues arising in major litigation, investigations, regulatory actions, and transactions.

Both Paczosa and Peruchini work with corporate executives and attorneys from leading law firms to identify and understand market risks, then develop innovative solutions for these complex issues, in both domestic and international matters.

Index